Astaganaga

33 1/3 Global

33 1/3 Global, a series related to but independent from **33 1/3**, takes the format of the original series of short, music-based books and brings the focus to music throughout the world. With initial volumes focusing on Japanese and Brazilian music, the series will also include volumes on the popular music of Australia/Oceania, Europe, Africa, the Middle East, and more.

33 1/3 Japan

Series Editor: Noriko Manabe

Spanning a range of artists and genres—from the 1970s rock of Happy End to technopop band Yellow Magic Orchestra, the Shibuya-kei of Cornelius, classic anime series *Cowboy Bebop,* J-Pop/EDM hybrid Perfume, and vocaloid star Hatsune Miku—**33 1/3 Japan** is a series devoted to in-depth examination of Japanese popular music of the twentieth and twenty-first centuries.

Published Titles:
Supercell's *Supercell* by Keisuke Yamada
Yoko Kanno's *Cowboy Bebop Soundtrack* by Rose Bridges
Perfume's *Game* by Patrick St. Michel
Cornelius's *Fantasma* by Martin Roberts
Joe Hisaishi's *My Neighbor Totoro: Soundtrack* by Kunio Hara
Shonen Knife's *Happy Hour* by Brooke McCorkle
Nenes' *Koza Dabasa* by Henry Johnson
Yuming's *The 14th Moon* by Lasse Lehtonen

Forthcoming Titles:
Yellow Magic Orchestra's *Yellow Magic Orchestra* by Toshiyuki Ohwada
Kohaku utagassen: The Red and White Song Contest by Shelley Brunt

33 1/3 Brazil

Series Editor: Jason Stanyek

Covering the genres of samba, tropicália, rock, hip hop, forró, bossa nova, heavy metal and funk, among others, **33 1/3 Brazil** is a series devoted to in-depth examination of the most important Brazilian albums of the twentieth and twenty-first centuries.

Published Titles:

Caetano Veloso's *A Foreign Sound* by Barbara Browning
Tim Maia's *Tim Maia Racional Vols. 1 &2* by Allen Thayer
João Gilberto and Stan Getz's *Getz/Gilberto* by Brian McCann
Gilberto Gil's *Refazenda* by Marc A. Hertzman
Dona Ivone Lara's *Sorriso Negro* by Mila Burns
Milton Nascimento and Lô Borges's *The Corner Club* by Jonathon Grasse
Racionais MCs' *Sobrevivendo no Inferno* by Derek Pardue
Naná Vasconcelos's *Saudades* by Daniel B. Sharp
Chico Buarque's First *Chico Buarque* by Charles A. Perrone

Forthcoming Titles:
Jorge Ben Jor's *África Brasil* by Frederick J. Moehn

33 1/3 Europe

Series Editor: Fabian Holt

Spanning a range of artists and genres, **33 1/3 Europe** offers engaging accounts of popular and culturally significant albums of Continental Europe and the North Atlantic from the twentieth and twenty-first centuries.

Published Titles:

Darkthrone's *A Blaze in the Northern Sky* by Ross Hagen
Ivo Papazov's *Balkanology* by Carol Silverman
Heiner Müller and Heiner Goebbels's *Wolokolamsker Chaussee* by Philip V. Bohlman
Modeselektor's *Happy Birthday!* by Sean Nye
Mercyful Fate's *Don't Break the Oath* by Henrik Marstal
Bea Playa's *I'll Be Your Plaything* by Anna Szemere and András Rónai
Various Artists' *DJs do Guetto* by Richard Elliott
Czesław Niemen's *Niemen Enigmatic* by Ewa Mazierska and Mariusz Gradowski
Massada's *Astaganaga* by Lutgard Mutsaers

Forthcoming Titles:
Los Rodriguez's *Sin Documentos* by Fernán del Val and Héctor Fouce
Nuovo Canzoniere Italiano's *Bella Ciao* by Jacopo Tomatis

Amália Rodrigues's *Amália at the Olympia* by Lilla Ellen Gray
Ardit Gjebrea's *Projekt Jon* by Nicholas Tochka
Vopli Vidopliassova's *Tantsi* by Maria Sonevytsky
Édith Piaf's *Recital 1961* by David Looseley
Iannis Xenakis' *Persepolis* by Aram Yardumian

33 1/3 Oceania

Series Editors: Jon Stratton (senior editor) and Jon Dale (specializing in books on albums from Aotearoa/New Zealand)

Spanning a range of artists and genres from Australian Indigenous artists to Maori and Pasifika artists, from Aotearoa/New Zealand noise music to Australian rock, and including music from Papua and other Pacific islands, **33 1/3 Oceania** offers exciting accounts of albums that illustrate the wide range of music made in the Oceania region.

Published Titles:
John Farnham's *Whispering Jack* by Graeme Turner
The Church's *Starfish* by Chris Gibson
Regurgitator's *Unit* by Lachlan Goold and Lauren Istvandity

Forthcoming Titles:
Ed Kuepper's *Honey Steel's Gold* by John Encarnacao
Kylie Minogue's *Kylie* by Adrian Renzo and Liz Giuffre
Space Waltz's *Space Waltz* by Ian Chapman
The Dead C's *Clyma est mort* by Darren Jorgensen
Chain's *Toward the Blues* by Peter Beilharz
Bic Runga's *The Drive* by Henry Johnson
The Front Lawn's *Songs from the Front Lawn* by Matthew Bannister

Astaganaga

Lutgard Mutsaers

Series Editor: Fabian Holt

BLOOMSBURY ACADEMIC
NEW YORK • LONDON • OXFORD • NEW DELHI • SYDNEY

BLOOMSBURY ACADEMIC
Bloomsbury Publishing Inc
1385 Broadway, New York, NY 10018, USA
50 Bedford Square, London, WC1B 3DP, UK
29 Earlsfort Terrace, Dublin 2, Ireland

BLOOMSBURY, BLOOMSBURY ACADEMIC and the Diana logo are trademarks of Bloomsbury Publishing Plc

First published in the United States of America 2023

Copyright © Lutgard Mutsaers, 2023

For legal purposes the Acknowledgments on p. 88 constitute an extension of this copyright page.

Cover credit: 333sound.com

All rights reserved. No part of this publication may be reproduced or transmitted in any form or by any means, electronic or mechanical, including photocopying, recording, or any information storage or retrieval system, without prior permission in writing from the publishers.

Bloomsbury Publishing Inc does not have any control over, or responsibility for, any third-party websites referred to or in this book. All internet addresses given in this book were correct at the time of going to press. The author and publisher regret any inconvenience caused if addresses have changed or sites have ceased to exist, but can accept no responsibility for any such changes.

Whilst every effort has been made to locate copyright holders the publishers would be grateful to hear from any person(s) not here acknowledged.

Library of Congress Cataloging-in-Publication Data
Names: Mutsaers, Lutgard, 1953- author.
Title: Astaganaga / Lutgard Mutsaers.
Description: [1st.] | New York, NY: Bloomsbury Academic, 2022. | Series: 33 1/3 Europe | Includes bibliographical references and index. | Summary: "The story about and behind the legendary 1978 debut album by first-generation Moluccan musicians raised in postcolonial Holland"– Provided by publisher.
Identifiers: LCCN 2022009682 (print) | LCCN 2022009683 (ebook) | ISBN 9781501372575 (hardback) | ISBN 9781501372568 (paperback) | ISBN 9781501372582 (epub) | ISBN 9781501372599 (pdf) | ISBN 9781501372605
Subjects: LCSH: Massada (Musical group). Astaganaga. | Massada (Musical group) | Rock music–Netherlands–History and criticism. | Popular music–Netherlands–Latin American influences. | Moluccans–Netherlands–Music–History and criticism.
Classification: LCC ML421.M4117 M88 2022 (print) | LCC ML421.M4117 (ebook) | DDC 782.42166092/2–dc23/eng/20220414
LC record available at https://lccn.loc.gov/2022009682
LC ebook record available at https://lccn.loc.gov/2022009683

ISBN: HB: 978-1-5013-7257-5
PB: 978-1-5013-7256-8
ePDF: 978-1-5013-7259-9
eBook: 978-1-5013-7258-2

Typeset by Deanta Global Publishing Services, Chennai, India
Printed and bound in Great Britain

Series: 33 1/3 Europe

To find out more about our authors and books visit www.bloomsbury.com and sign up for our newsletters.

Contents

Introduction 1

Part I Backdrops 5

    Colonial Times and Impact 5
    Popular Music in Exile 10
    Latin in the Lowlands 17

Part II Massada before *Astaganaga* 23

    In the Air 23
    What's in a Name 27
    Decisive Break 29
    The Action Years 32

Part III Massada's *Astaganaga* 41

    The Making Of 41
    Track by Track 46
    Sleeve Art and Credits 49
    Reception and Rewards 51

Part IV Massada after *Astaganaga* 65

    Bang the Drum 65
    Mission Accomplished 67
    Full Circle 74
    Hindsight 76

Part V Afterwork 79

    Discography 79
    About Research 80

Sources and Literature 81
Part I Backdrops 82
Part II Massada before *Astaganaga* 86
Part III Massada's *Astaganaga* 87
Part IV Massada after *Astaganaga* 87
Acknowledgments 88
About the Author 88

Notes 89
Index 97

Introduction

Astaganaga by Massada holds a unique place in the realm of popular music made in the Netherlands. Released in May 1978 on an independent Dutch label, the album landed in the aftermath of a traumatizing episode for the nation at large. A small number of radicalized young people with firearms and a political agenda had occupied buildings and hijacked trains. Their actions had turned violent and had cost lives. The news had been all over the national and international media.

Worldwide the increase of death-defying actions to draw the general public's attention to some minority cause, partisan ideal, or liberation movement was a sign of the times. The Netherlands had no recent experience of the kind. All the more confrontational was the wake-up call to the home consequences of the nation's colonial past. Massada's rise as a live band and the reception of their debut studio album *Astaganaga* were inextricably linked to the postcolonial issue at stake.

Massada self-identified as a Moluccan band. Most members had been born and/or raised in the close-knit South East Asian community in the Netherlands that had produced the action takers. The general public therefore automatically perceived the band as a fearsome bunch of rebels with a cause—which in the rock world was something to be. To questions about their political allegiances Massada's musicians stoically replied that they were only in it for the music. Today *Astaganaga* is an artful witness to a bygone era of shattered illusions, failing integration, and general mistrust. At the time of release *Astaganaga* sent an empowering message of awareness and encouragement. Without so many words Massada had seized the moment.

Between 1975 and 1980 Massada was a force to reckon with. In 1975 the music press first noticed the band. In 1980 Massada had their first number one in the singles chart. In these years of maximum exposure Massada played hundreds of gigs, produced two critically acclaimed and commercially successful albums, went international, received prestigious awards, and emerged apparently unscathed from a sudden breakup. After the reshuffle the decline of Massada's cultural urgency and national relevance was rapid.

By adding their own spice to the internationally popular mix of percussive rhythms and flowing melodies over a basic rock sound—Santana (United States) was a fitting reference— Massada created their own signature sound. *Astaganaga* not only was a welcome alternative to mainstream pop in the era of disco as a dominant international craze, but its release also marked a decisive moment in Dutch postcolonial politics. In 1978, the year of *Astaganaga*, the government ended all strictly political negotiations with the leaders of the Moluccan community. The contact and cooperation from then on would be limited to social and cultural topics and policies. *Astaganaga* was Massada's first cautious step into a musical world of engagement with Moluccan themes and issues without alienating their Dutch fanbase.

Massada entered the new millennium as a living legend. Now a rejuvenated revival orchestra with two original members, Massada preserves the uplifting repertoire and energetic sound that had made their name and solidified their reputation. Today *Astaganaga* has the stature of a true classic: the music transcends the limitations of time, space, and cultural conditioning and defies the gravity of its historical context.

Part I
Backdrops

The Moluccan community in the Netherlands came into being in 1951 with one stroke of a pen and the idle promise of a speedy return to their ancestral home in the South Moluccan archipelago. The generation born and/or raised in the Netherlands had to come to terms with the frustration and homesickness of their parents. Massada was a voice of that generation.

Colonial Times and Impact

In the early 1600s Protestant Christian Dutch settlers and traders secured their first stronghold in South East Asia by expelling their Catholic Portuguese predecessors from Amboina (now Ambon City) on Ambon Island in the center of the economically interesting South Moluccan archipelago, or Spice Islands as they were nicknamed for their valuable yield of cloves, mace, and nutmeg. Soon after planting their flag the Dutch relocated to new-built Batavia (now Jakarta) on the island of Java. The Spice Islands were reduced to production sites for the Dutch East India Company, their native populations exploited and impoverished or expelled and replaced by an imported workforce of enslaved individuals. Indonesia's first officially recognized freedom fighter Thomas Matulessy alias Pattimura (1782–1817) came from Ambon's neighboring island Saparua. By that time the Dutch East India Company was bankrupt and the Netherlands had been reinvented as a kingdom ruled by the House of Orange.

In the course of the nineteenth century the Dutch rolled out their system of colonization. Expansion and control were important aspects of Dutch domination. To this end the Royal Dutch East Indies Army KNIL (*Koninklijk Nederlands-Indisch Leger*) hired free natives into its lower ranks. Protestant Christian men from the Moluccan Islands formed a special contingent for sharing the minority religion of the ruling class against a vast majority of Muslims, Hindus, and animists. The army took them away from home, often for life. With their wives they lived in military barrack camps. Their children were literally born into KNIL culture.

Not all baptized Moluccans opted for an army job. Many left their home islands to pursue the schooling necessary for promotion in the colonial ranks. On the basis of professional achievements some of them successfully petitioned for a legal status equal to that of Indo-Europeans who were privileged by birth. To Moluccans working in and with the colonial system was a means to an end. The end was to save some money and go home.

Away from home Moluccans cultivated their sense of community and identity in their own professional organizations, social clubs, and sports teams. On all levels of competition they used their rallying slogan *mena muria*, "all for one and one for all." The slogan originated in the ancient tribal practice of rowing exactly in time in wooden *arumbai* (fishing boats) for maximum speed. The ultimate addition to Moluccan organizations was the founding in 1935 of the *Geredja Protestan Maluku* (Moluccan Protestant Church). By that time their community had already developed a fixed stage format of "typically" Moluccan entertainment for mixed crowds at *pasar malam* (evening markets) and theaters in the urban centers of the colony. Songs of longing for home and praise of the natural beauty of Maluku formed a substantial part of the repertoire.

The political events of the 1940s determined the fate of Moluccan KNIL-employees and their families. During the Indonesian War of Independence (1945–9) the Moluccan KNIL-contingent sided with the Dutch. This is why their lives were expected to be in danger in the newborn state. Their safety was a concern of the Dutch on their way out. A complicating factor was the proclamation of the *Republik Maluku Selatan* (Republic of the South Moluccas) RMS on April 25, 1950.

After the dissolution of the KNIL in July 1950 on Java the former Moluccan contingent and their families longed to go home, but the Indonesian army had already sealed off the RMS territory. The Dutch government wanted diplomatic and trade relations with the central(ized) Indonesian government and therefore needed to distance itself from the RMS. Around 4,000 former KNIL-employees of Moluccan descent had already been rehired into the Royal Dutch Army. They received the order—others claim they went voluntarily—to embark for the Netherlands, together with their wives and children, as a temporary solution to the personal danger they faced.

Between March and June 1951 around 12,500 people were transferred by ocean liners for an expected sojourn of six months at most, in any case until a safe return could be guaranteed. Back home the worst-case scenario was unfurling. The Indonesian army crushed the RMS militia. Undaunted, the leaders regrouped their followers in the jungle of Ceram and started a guerilla.

On arrival in the Netherlands the men already knew or learned they were collectively discharged from the Royal Dutch Army and had lost all rights attached to the job.[1] The fact would go down in exile folklore and literature as the Big Betrayal. The transferees were divided into groups and transported to dozens of derelict relief camps, empty convents, and other facilities of a temporary nature on the outskirts of towns and villages at considerable distances from one another. Some sites had lately been used as prison or transit camps and juvenile reform centers. With their watchtowers and barbed wire these creepy places were begging for demolition. Instead, they indefinitely turned into the home from home for a part of the transferred group.

On top of the hurt of the betrayal, the lack of perspective, and total unfamiliarity with country, climate, and culture the list of formal restrictions and casual humiliations was endless. Against all odds, most transferees managed to keep their dream alive. To the outside world they showed a united front. A majority preserved their language and customs, followed the leaders of the RMS government in exile, and attended the Moluccan Protestant Church in exile. Their children went to Dutch schools, learned the language, made friends, but the education system tended to underestimate their potential and steer them into menial jobs or domestic work.

In 1963 the transferees were informed by their leaders that they had lost their automatically obtained Indonesian nationality for having overstayed the legal term of their absence. In December 1963 the Indonesian government arrested RMS president and jungle commando leader Chris Soumokil. The dream was falling apart. Soumokil's followers in exile refused to be naturalized as Dutch citizens, resisted the planned integration into Dutch society, and rejected the idea of assimilation. The execution in 1966 of Soumokil as a political prisoner of the new Suharto regime made large numbers of followers in exile take to the streets in anger and protest. It triggered the process of radicalization within the community's young generation. Soumokil's widow and their teenage son moved to the Netherlands where she reluctantly became the figurehead of the Moluccan movement for independence and he grew up to be an activist.[2]

In 1970 the Dutch government ordered the demolition of the remaining barrack camps and the rehousing of the families in designated areas of towns and villages where other families already had moved to. For the militant among the generation of 1951, this was one imperative to many. Their individual resistance was met with police force and fire hoses. The authorities in the meantime ignored the importance of semantics by continuing to use the colonial term "Ambonese," implying inequality and subordination while playing on old-time loyalty. The war of words was part of the painstaking decolonizing process of the former colonizer.

The 1970s was the decade of the generation born and/or raised in the camps, the generation that was bound to collectively internalize the built-up frustration and sorrow of their parents while individually pursuing their own dreams and goals. They were free to choose the context of their move forward. Society at large had long-lost interest in Moluccan issues. Youth culture in the 1960s had speeded up the process of secularization and stimulated emancipation movements. Amsterdam was the self-proclaimed magical center of the world. The capital attracted young people from all over the world. For performers and audiences of contemporary jazz, rock, and fusion Amsterdam was the place to be.

Popular Music in Exile

Rewind to 1951. Among the Moluccan transferees arriving in the Netherlands on March 21, 1951, with the first ship were the parents of Johnny Manuhutu (1948; Cirebon, Java), future founding member of Massada.[3] At the time of arrival Johnny was two and a half years old. From this first group 192 persons belonging to 60 nuclear families were taken to Camp Almere on the wooded outskirts of Huizen, a sleepy village some 25 kilometers southeast of Amsterdam. Camp Almere had recently served as a reform site for juvenile delinquents and children of wartime collaborators.

A local committee of lady volunteers immediately started to collect warm clothes, shoes, baby cribs, and whatever else was needed on top of the bare essentials already provided for. Leny Grondel-Chotzen (1893–1988) was the driving force of the charity group. A first-generation Dutch national of Eastern-European Jewish descent—her parents had fled the pogroms of the Russian Empire—she had experienced personal traumas and losses during the Nazi occupation of the Netherlands. After the war she became involved in the humanist movement. Mrs.

Grondel visited Camp Almere shortly after the arrival of the temporary inhabitants. She knew it was important also to look after immaterial needs. So she raised funds for the purchase of musical instruments.

Before long the camp had its own band with up to twenty string players—guitars, ukuleles, mandolins, and an electrical Hawaiian guitar connected to a radio amp—led by Nico Patty.[4] Mrs. Grondel took the band on the road to other camps because the Moluccans were not allowed to travel unchaperoned. She rang venues and social clubs and asked, demanded, to book the band and drum up a full house for fundraising purposes. Her numerous initiatives, also for the women and children in the camp, gained her the nickname *Ibu Maluku*, Mother of the Moluccans. The example of Camp Almere was soon followed elsewhere. At public performances of Moluccan bands Dutch spectators applauded the songs and dances of Moluccan folklore, like they would have done in colonial times. But when the bands played typically Dutch songs such as the national anthem and popular standards, they were likely to meet disapproval.[5]

The unwritten code of apartheid did not pertain to international (i.e., American) popular music. The genre popular with Moluccan musicians in exile was Hawaiian. Hawaiian had reached the urban centers of the Dutch East Indies shortly after the genre had been exposed, literally, at the World's Fair of 1915 in San Francisco. Hula dancing became all the rage. At the time Hawaii was a US protectorate. Hawaiian bands had access to the US circuit of traveling tent shows or "wheels." The peculiar sound that resulted from sliding a bottleneck, comb, or metal bar over the frets of a Spanish guitar was widely copied and integrated into folk genres such as country music and rural blues and influenced commercial songwriting and recording.

Hawaiian came to the Dutch East Indies as showbiz Hawaiian, a theatrical genre, a music for performers, male and female, to dress up for and for listeners to look at. As showbiz thrives on stereotypes, Hawaiian came closest to authenticity when performed by Polynesian islanders. Moluccans were the Polynesian islanders of the Dutch East Indies. Another factor that bound Hawaiians and Moluccans was the enduring Portuguese influence in both cultures. Moluccan musicians took to Hawaiian for the entertainment of the colonial upper class. Their repertoire consisted of popular Hawaiian tunes in commercial rotation plus traditional Moluccan folk songs (*lagu-lagu*) and dance tunes for women and men separately. Audiences in the colony therefore associated Hawaiian first of all with Moluccan musicians, singers, and dancers.

In the Netherlands, Hawaiian had one epicenter in The Hague, the city where colonial officials used to spend their leave, and another in Rotterdam, where sailors found entertainment in bars and brothels. The genre more or less escaped the wartime ban of all things American or allied, even when accomplished jazz musicians found temporary refuge in amateur Hawaiian ensembles and in return enriched the sound and raised the quality bar. Key to the fusion of jazz and Hawaiian was the sound of the Hawaiian guitar as a solo instrument.

The Honolulu Queens came on the scene in The Hague in 1939. They were a trio of Moluccan sisters whose father, an aficionado of real (uncommercialized) Hawaiian, was on extended leave. They performed all through the war years and left a handful of recordings of self-penned songs with Dutch lyrics. The homegrown Kilima Hawaiians from Rotterdam formed the commercial tip of the Hawaiian iceberg. Their top years (records, radio, shows) coincided with the last Dutch colonial war (1945–9). In the 1950s, Hawaiian worked miracles as a sound of nostalgia for the population at large and around 330,000 Indo-European (so called) repatriates from Indonesia. Here was a market. That market was not automatically open to Moluccans of the camps.

Rudi Wairata (1929–81) was born on the North Moluccan island of Ternate. His family moved to Java when he was eleven. Wairata was in his late teens when he made his radio debut as a Hawaiian guitarist at the Dutch East Indies Broadcasting Organization NIROM. Through his father's contacts he obtained a scholarship to the Royal Conservatory in The Hague. In 1950 Wairata arrived in the Netherlands. He never planned a musical career there, but the postcolonial market for Hawaiian changed his perspective. In 1951 he joined the Mena Moeria Minstrels—the traditional Maluku motto in Dutch spelling combined with the American trade term for show people—and started his professional career as a musician and bandleader. With the Mena Moeria Minstrels, the Hawaiian Minstrels, the Amboina Serenaders, and the New Polynesians he played background music in restaurants and hotel lobbies, performed for Dutch radio, made records for the Dutch label Omega (Dureco), and toured. He married a Dutch singer who made a name for herself as Ann Wairata.

In 1958 the arrival in the Netherlands of the famous Moluccan Hawaiian guitarist George De Fretes (1921–81)—who made his passage from Indonesia as a stowaway, was discovered at sea and started his Dutch sojourn in jail as an illegal immigrant—exposed Wairata as an unauthorized performer, live and on record, of compositions copyrighted by De Fretes. The Dutch firm Phonogram took care of business and recorded De Fretes and his Royal Hawaiian Minstrels in his own repertoire. Too late though for commercial success. Rock and roll had arrived.

Wairata had been the first to pick up on the new trend with his Omega single "Honolulu Rock-a Roll-a", an A-side, and his RCA single "Rock and Roll and Breezes", a B-side, both 78 RPMs released in 1956. His fusion sounded too much like pop Hawaiian and pastiche to pass for generic rock and roll, but it is indicative of the necessity for professional musicians in the entertainment world to keep up with the latest trends. Rock and roll clearly was not a suitable style to musically update Moluccan folk songs. These songs remained in the camps and only came out at folkloric occasions such as the postwar Dutch circuit of *pasar malam* colonial style.

Rock and roll was the springboard of electric guitarists and drummers. On stage rock and roll was almost entirely an amateur activity of young male Indo-European repatriates in cities with open youth clubs and music cafés. They created a niche of their own. The groundbreaking movement (1956–64) was retrospectively labeled "indorock" by a Dutch record collector. The label stuck as an umbrella term for rock and roll bands of, or dominated in number by musicians born and raised in Indonesia. Musically it would be more appropriate to speak of indorock-and-roll as a more or less distinguishable branch of the genre made in the United States.

When indorock-and-roll was hip and happening the genre was ignored by the Dutch media. There were hundreds of bands. A dozen top groups found well-paid employment in West-German clubs frequented by American and British military personnel of the occupying peace forces. There the self-taught musicians learned how to dress for the stage, make shows, and play dance music for hours on end. The temporary presence of Elvis Presley as a private in the American zone added to the excitement of being a rock and roll band there and then. Upon return they showed off their second-hand American cars and bling jewelry.

In the Moluccan camps rock and roll fans picked up electric guitars and drum sticks and started their own bands with brothers, nephews, and friends. They rehearsed in the community center of the camp and played at Moluccan parties and weddings. Very few bands managed to build a following outside. Outside indorock-and-roll dominated the field. The proverbial exception was The Black Magic from Camp Plasmolen near Mook. The band owed their reputation to their star Max Tahalele (1944–2005), a guitar legend who posthumously had a street in his longtime hometown Nijmegen named after him.

In 1963, fifteen-year-old Johnny Manuhutu of Camp Almere started a band with boys from the camp. They named themselves The Eagles after the mythical *garuda* of South East Asian folklore. Johnny played guitar and sang. Usje Sabandar (1949; Cimahi, Java) played bass guitar. Band members came and went. They played for fun and friends. Around 1967 Chris Latul joined as lead guitarist. He took the band one step further.

Chris Latul was born in 1948 in Surabaya, Java. His father was a telegraphist officer of the colonial navy. In 1951 he took his family to the Netherlands on the first transfer ship with former KNIL personnel. The navy families ended up in decent housing in and around the naval base of Den Helder. The Latul family was housed in the village of Medemblik. That same year father Latul took his leave from the Dutch navy and moved his family to Dutch New Guinea, which had remained a part of the Dutch East Indies, on KLM's maiden flight from Amsterdam to Sydney.[6]

Chris grew up with the expectation that Dutch New Guinea was soon to gain its independence. They already had their own flag and their own national anthem. The Republic of Indonesia, however, was determined to annex the last colonial Dutch province. The Dutch government in turn was determined not to let the story of Maluku repeat itself. In 1962 the Netherlands handed Dutch New Guinea over to the Republic of Indonesia.

Father Latul immediately took his family to the Netherlands, this time for good. For the better part of the 1960s, the family lived in Amsterdam close to the Concertgebouw. Amsterdam was as much the Netherlands as New York was the United States. In the 1960s hip Amsterdam reinvented their city as the magical center of the world. Pop art, new jazz, modern dance—if it did not happen in Amsterdam it did not exist.

At fourteen, Chris had started to play electric guitar by listening to and learning from the records of the popular British guitar band The Shadows with lead guitarist Hank B. Marvin. Their interpretation of the instrumental surf sound of The Ventures (US) had developed into a sophisticated style of their own. The Shadows were big in the Netherlands when Chris picked up his guitar. The Ventures had already worked their influence on indorock-and-roll as a distinct style developed in the Netherlands. The electric guitar as a lead instrument, two or more lead guitars dueling, bass guitarists responding with melody lines, rhythm guitarists teaming up with drummers: the creative space of rock and roll was largely owned by newcomers to Dutch culture before British Beat invaded in 1964. At that point, the natives stepped in and took over.

For a while the Latul family lived in Eemnes, a village close to Huizen and Camp Almere where Chris met Johnny Manuhutu who asked him to join The Eagles. Chris had no personal experience of camp life and inflammable ex-KNIL frustrations, but he understood the feeling of betrayal the parent generation was suffering from and unwillingly burdened their children with. With Chris on board and Johnny focusing on lead vocals, The Eagles were ready to perform in front of peers getting together for the music itself. Songwriting in the meantime had become part of the basic requirements for any band that wanted to be taken seriously. As soon as Chris discovered the music of Santana with lead guitarist Carlos Santana he was hooked. He steered The Eagles into latinrock US style, a new live sound in the Netherlands.

Latin in the Lowlands

In 1950s Dutch culture, the term "latin" referred to ballroom and social dancing styles associated with South American countries and popularized through Hollywood movies and commercial recordings. Dancing schools were teaching the cha-cha-cha, the mambo, and the rumba. Compared to the usual waltzes and foxtrots for social gatherings, the novelty of latin was in the rhythms of the percussion instruments and the sound of Spanish guitars. When latin came to the Netherlands, the Dutch link with South America and the Caribbean was colonial: continental Surinam and a group of Antillean islands together formed the Dutch West Indies.

The combination of live rock and roll and latin dance rhythms was pioneered by indorock-and-roll bands at Saturday night dances of dancing schools and youth clubs. Out of this scene came Electric Johnny and His Skyrockets.[7] By 1960 the Rotterdam-based group consisted of seven musicians: four electric guitarists, a bass guitarist, a drummer, and a percussionist on bongos, maracas, claves, and guiro. They developed their own brand of latin percussion indorock-and-roll in their renditions of popular ballroom tunes such as "Begin The Beguine" and "Carioca". Their EPs *South American Rock Volume I* (1960) and *South American Rock Volume II* (1961) for the Dutch firm CNR were commercial successes at home and abroad, including the United States, the United Kingdom, Scandinavia, and France. The band toured extensively.

Like anywhere else the international twist craze of the early 1960s changed the face of dancing to popular music in the Netherlands in a revolutionary way. When the craze as such was over there were no more compelling rules and regulations in steps and movements across the dancefloor, no more fixed moments to begin and end a dance. Not even a dancing partner was required anymore. Twist music was the last flare-up of rock and roll and therefore of indorock-and-roll. Later in the decade British beat groups, bluesrock bands, and Dylan-epigones invested in lyrics. They wanted their fans to listen to what they had to say. Music for dancing fell out of grace with the rock generation that subscribed to the rock magazines that dictated proper taste in rock.

Latin came back with a vengeance in the adventurous jazz scene of Amsterdam at home in the Paradiso. Opened in 1968 as a progressive youth club and venue for contemporary music, the Paradiso was the place where tenorsaxofonist Hans Dulfer programmed his weekly Jazz Nights. In 1969, Dulfer caused a small sensation with his new multicultural band Ritmo Natural. The group pioneered their own blend of Afro-Caribbean cross rhythms with jazz improvisation, swing, and what Dulfer called "heavy soul," referring to the raw sound of US rhythm and blues with horns. Conga and timbales player with Ritmo Natural was Steve Boston (1935–2017), later nicknamed Godfather of Dutch Percussionists.[8]

Boston had moved from Surinam to Amsterdam in the mid-1950s. He joined the scene in and around Club Tropicana where latin dance music was the thing. With Heavy Soul Inc., the band that preceded Ritmo Natural, Boston played the 1969 Montreux Jazz Festival. Montreux had just opened its doors to rock. Two British bands walked in: progressive rockers Colosseum and bluesrockers Ten Year After. The electric guitar had arrived on the European jazz stage as a lead instrument of fusion styles. That same year Santana introduced their brand of latin percussion rock to the crowd at the Woodstock festival. Over the next three years Ritmo Natural was the big name in latin percussion jazz made in the Netherlands. In the 1971 popularity poll of the Dutch magazine *Jazzwereld* (Jazz World) Ritmo Natural came out on top.

The coming man in the Amsterdam jazz and improvisation scene of the early 1970s was the Japanese-Indonesian percussionist Nippy Noya.[9] He was five years old when his adoptive Moluccan ex-KNIL family had taken him to the Netherlands. He grew up in Camp Schattenberg (part of former concentration camp Westerbork) near Assen. Like elsewhere music was part of camp life. When Nippy heard records of latin dance music, he hooked on to the sound of congas. He did not think of a career as a musician until 1970 when he saw Ritmo Natural at the Paradiso. After the concert he approached Steven Boston and asked him where he might find a set of congas for sale. Boston gave him the address of a Surinamese friend in Amsterdam. It all went from there.

After Boston had left Ritmo Natural, Dulfer called Noya for a gig at the Newport Jazz In Holland festival in Rotterdam in 1973 (on the bill were, among others, Sarah Vaughan, Miles Davis, Duke Ellington, and B. B. King). Through a Dutch agency in the rock and pop world, Noya was already making a living as a freelance percussionist with successful acts. "A prodigy of latin percussion," a national newspaper called him.[10]

The secret of his inimitable personal style was, in his own words, "the fact that I don't have a culture, pride and tradition of my own."[11] He explained he did not share the background of Afro-American or Latino-American musicians. And with due respect for his Moluccan upbringing, he remained a relative outsider of their culture, pride, and tradition as well. This awareness gave him the freedom to go his own way. Noya departed with nothing in terms of musical schooling. He consciously avoided the influences that came with listening to records. His inspiration came from the mood of the music he was invited to contribute to and the connection with his fellow musicians, regardless of genre or entourage.

In between paid jobs at home and abroad, Nippy was with The Eagles from Camp Almere in their run-up to becoming Massada.

Part II
Massada before *Astaganaga*

Latin rock was a novel sound in international popular music when The Eagles changed their name to Massada. Their Dutch manager sent them on a three months promotion tour around youth clubs and rock venues. At the Amsterdam Paradiso their decisive break took place. *Muziekkrant Oor*, the Dutch equivalent of *Rolling Stone*, introduced Massada to its critical constituency. The actions of militant Moluccans forced Massada to operate in a politicized context.

In the Air

The commercial top in latin pop/rock in the early 1970s was Santana, the band from San Francisco led by the Mexican-American guitarist Carlos Santana. At the Woodstock festival (1969) Santana had stunned the crowd with their unleashed performance of latin percussion rock. Their first album *Santana* (1969) rode the wave of their Woodstock fame. By the time the documentary film *Woodstock* (1970) reached Dutch cinemas Santana already had a fanbase in the Netherlands. On June

26, 1970, Santana performed at the Holland Pop Festival, nicknamed Dutch Woodstock.[1] Their second album *Abraxas* (1970) broke all records. Santana's rocked-up rendition of Tito Puente's "Oye Como Va" (1962) fed an international taste for the dance music of Puerto Rican and Cuban immigrants in Spanish Harlem, New York.

On their European tours in the 1970s Santana always visited the Netherlands for at least one concert in a large hall. Dutch rockfans were just beginning to get used to live performances of American superstars. Seeing top latin percussionists at work was especially fascinating. The craft was new to most Dutch eyes and ears. Also, the physical sensation was new. Santana's hits were played on prime-time public radio, commercial Radio Luxemburg, and pirate pop stations, but there was nothing like a live show. Santana was particularly popular with Moluccan teenagers, especially the relatively big number of guitarists in the community.[2]

The appreciation of the style was not limited to Santana. In fact, an entire movement of creative musicians in and around San Francisco was delivering the sound of their time and place with the urgency of a political movement. The movement's alternative (non-mainstream and yet popular) sound inspired The Eagles on their way to becoming Massada. One of the relevant names was Malo with guitarist Jorge Santana, brother of Carlos. In Curaçao in the Caribbean part of the Netherlands, Malo in 1972 had a hit with their first single "Suavecito"/"Nena". "Suavecito" landed in the repertoire of many a local band as a staple of the cruising sound for slow dancing. "Nena" had the latin boogaloo groove popular with the budding disco scene. Later, when Massada already had two albums out, the

Dutch-Antillean newspaper *Amigoe* pointed at the "vague" influences of Santana and Malo in Massada's music.[3] By that time "Nena" was an audiences' favorite in Massada's live repertoire.

The story of Malo has interesting parallels with the story of Massada. Both groups had a close connection to an immigrant community keen on displaying and celebrating their exile culture with the means and media available at their place of arrival. Around 1970 Jorge Santana (1951–2020) became actively involved in the South American immigrant community in the San Francisco Mission District. Focal point of the district was the *Galería De La Raza* (Gallery of the Race), founded in 1970 as a meeting point, music venue, art gallery, and debating site for the Spanish-speaking Latino community in general and the Chicano community of Mexican immigrants in particular. The music of Malo was a prominent part of the soundtrack to the *Chicano Power!* movement around *La Raza*.

When Malo broke up in 1974 they left four albums, all with major record company Warner Bros. Their debut *Malo* (1972) was their most successful one. It reached no. 14 in the US Top 200 Album Charts. The colorful sleeve shows a collage of pre-Columbian human figures and symbols, a trend that tied in with the philosophy of *La Raza*. Malo and other top groups of the movement such as Chango, El Chicano, and Azteca were later compiled under the heading *Chicano Power! 1968-1976*. Dakila had a special place in the movement. The band consisted of musicians from the Philippines, the longtime Spanish colony in the Pacific that had been sold to the United States in 1898 and in 1946 had gained independence. *Dakila*

(1972) is their only album. They sang in English, Spanish, and the indigenous Filippino language Tagalog.

Searching for roots and displaying those roots in a topical way was an integral part of the *Chicano Power!* movement. Being away from home permanently, for reasons beyond the strictly personal, with music as their means of expression and bridge to society at large resembled the situation of the band that was to be Massada. Dakila, Malo, and other members of the movement stayed away from obvious protest songs. They wrote about matters of the heart, about dancing as a metaphor for sexual desire from the macho perspective of their culture, and about having a good time and getting away from everyday worries, as Massada would. The protest was implicit but the message was taken nevertheless. Rock was a rebel sound in itself, a cry for change. The fans knew. Insiders of the culture knew about pride and tradition. The music was for everyone to enjoy.

Around the same time the UK showband Osibisa came from another direction with a similar sound built on rock and percussion. The group consisted of musicians with backgrounds in Ghana, Nigeria, and the former British West Indies isles of Trinidad, Antigua, and Grenada. Their sound was made up of electric guitar, bass guitar, drums, percussion, keyboards, flute/tenor saxophone, and trumpet/flugelhorn. The percussion element was especially strong in the instrumental breaks, forecasting the evolution of disco into experimental hip hop tracks. They performed with naked upper bodies adorned with tribal paraphernalia.

"Crisscross rhythms that explode with happiness" was the newspaper header that announced Osibisa's debut on Dutch television in September 1971.[4] The band followed up with a tour and came back several times over the next few years. Their instrumentation, happy sound, percussion breaks, singalong hits, and stage looks gave The Eagles plenty of reference points and sources of inspiration when they were about to change their name to Massada.

What's in a Name

In 1970 the Dutch government decided to close the Moluccan camps and enforce a program of integration into Dutch society. The decision heralded a new era of protest and resistance in which the 1970s generation took the lead. Their focus was international. The founding of the United Nations Association of the Spice Islands (UNASI) in 1972 entailed the right to address the General Assembly of the UN. In a new sweep of enthusiasm for action, the RMS in exile had already founded its own youth organization.[5] Other youth organizations sprang up from within the community, each with its own program and agenda. The harvest of the cultural rejuvenation of the previous decade had begun.

The Eagles were first-hand witnesses. Under pressure, the last family of Camp Almere moved into the municipality of Huizen in 1972. The site was torn down immediately after. The only barrack left standing was the community center *Boenga Tjengkeh* (Clove Flower), the rehearsal space of The Eagles.[6] The band was allowed to go on using it, for the time being. In the spring of 1973, The Eagles from the United States had their breakthrough in the Netherlands with their second album *Desperado*, a top ten album for many weeks. The Eagles from Huizen had big ambitions of their own. With Johnny's younger brother Eppy Manuhutu (1952; Huizen) on drums and Nippy Noya as percussionist Johnny, Usje, and Chris had found the line-up and the sound they wanted. Their repertoire contained songs by, among others, Santana, Chicago (with the famous Brazilian percussionist Laudir de Oliveira), and the white Motown act Rare Earth. A cover band had no chance to make it beyond bars and nightclubs. Chris Latul provided the original compositions in the mix of styles The Eagles had mastered. For their next step they needed a new name.

In 1973 the name Massada resounded wide and far in another context. Masada (Oxford English spelling with one s) was the name of the ancient mountain fortress on the west bank of the Dead Sea in Israel. On the basis of recent excavations by archaeologists new assumptions had been made about the legendary last stand of the Jews against the Romans in the year 73. At Mount Masada a group of around 1,000 men, women, and children belonging to a local party of religious fanatics had taken refuge behind the walls of the fortress and met their untimely end there. The year 1973 saw an avalanche of books and exhibitions dedicated to Masada, focusing on stories of heroism and perseverance of the few against the many. The year 1973 also saw the Yom Kippur War of the young state of Israel against a coalition of Arab powers. Dutch media paid due attention to the anniversary of the Mount Masada story and its relevance in the here and now. The only newspaper that consistently reported about and in favor of the Moluccan cause—a fundamentally Protestant Christian medium spelled by secular and religious leaders in the community—spent no less than three page-long articles on the subject.[7]

The name Massada sent the unambiguous message of no surrender. Deeper layers of meaning have to do with language. In Malay, the lingua franca of South East Asia in colonial times, *masa* means time, *sada* means now. The time is now. Now is the time. In the modern lingua franca of Indonesia *masadah*, derived from the Portuguese word *maçada*, means trouble.

Decisive Break

Joke Zonneveld (1945) met Massada around the time of their first concert at De Melkweg in Amsterdam on April 6, 1974. The venue had just started as a multicultural and multidisciplinary club where groundbreaking audiovisual artists met an open-minded audience. In terms of importance for the progressive music scene De Melkweg came second only to the Paradiso. Nippy Noya had heard of Zonneveld through his expanding network as a freelance percussionist. She was the self-made manager of the hard-gigging Amsterdam-based rock band her British boyfriend was a member of, next to Herman Brood, Holland's own archetypical rock-and-roll junkie. Not prepared to take another act on board, she turned Massada down. When the rock band unexpectedly split and left her with already contracted dates she remembered Massada. The band already had a sound system of their own which they were paying for in installments.

Their first booking with Zonneveld took them to a university students' club in Utrecht on August 31, 1974. The punters expected to see the rock band. They got Massada. From there Zonneveld sent Massada into the open youth club circuit subsidized by local authorities from their budget for social work. The principal aim of the subsidy scheme was to keep adolescents from the streets and mischief. It would take another ten years for a selected rock/pop club circuit across the nation to be transferred to the arts budget.[8] In that process Amsterdam took the lead. In particular, at the Paradiso popular music was taken seriously as a contemporary art form. Any band in search of recognition in that field needed the Paradiso.

Zonneveld worked exclusively for Massada. She laid out a five-year plan and set targets. To begin with she sent them on a three months promotion tour, winning the public that had not been exposed yet to homegrown bands like Massada. Their financial strategy with Zonneveld was to keep investing their earnings in more and better gear, light, and transport until they had reached their first goal, the national top. At the end of the promotion tour Noya opted out. He had a young family of his own to support and received interesting offers elsewhere. At key moments in Massada's future career he would be there though.

The new percussionist was Zeth Mustamu. His mother had been pregnant with him when she and her ex-KNIL husband were transferred from Indonesia to the Netherlands in 1951. Zeth was born in Vlissingen. The Mustamu family settled outside the camp community at an early stage. Like Chris Latul, Zeth was college-educated. Among his heroes were the world-famous Nuyorican timbalero Tito Puente, whose records he studied meticulously, and the younger generation of innovative percussionists in latin rock, such as Mingo Lewis of Santana and Rudy Regalado of El Chicano. A true rhythm wizard and a magnetic stage personality Zeth Mustamu also contributed to the creative process. He would write Massada's signature tune "Latin Dance".

On Saturday night February 1, 1975, Massada played the Amsterdam rock temple Paradiso for the first time. Their friend and aspiring percussionist Dave Gervais joined them on tambourine and panflute. With their music loud and clear through twenty-two microphones, four amplifiers of 150 watt and two of 300 watt, and a colorful light show called Midnight Circus, Massada puzzled the house quite a bit. "One has to learn to understand this music," one newspaper commented.[9]

The invitation to join the roster of the *Nederlandse Groepenpresentatie* (Showdown of Dutch Bands) at the Paradiso on February 26 was a promise to catapult Massada into the scene of *Muziekkrant Oor* and associated radio deejays. The venue already was a fixed stopover for international acts. In the first half of the 1975 Fairport Convention, Judas Priest, Rufus & Chaka Khan and Steeleye Span, to name but a few, performed there. The *Groepenpresentatie*, a contest for up-and-coming bands, was a new format for the sort of venue the Paradiso was. Massada had brought their secret weapon, Nippy Noya. Part of their winning performance was broadcast on public radio a few days later.

Muziekkrant Oor sent a reporter to Zonneveld's place for an interview with Johnny Manuhutu and Chris Latul.[10] "We're often compared with Santana because we have more or less the same line-up and there are also latin influences in our music," said Chris, "but we have undergone other influences as well, I mean South Moluccan, and our music is a lot lighter [. . .] and a lot more focused on melody." Johnny underlined the social aspect of their music: "We want to entertain people, take them to another world so to speak. For instance, with the percussion instruments, it is very well possible to imitate jungle sounds, which make people happy and let them forget their sorrows. We want to make accessible music and not drown in egotrips and complexities." Both of them assured the interviewer that they did not want to cater to a select group of any kind.

On July 12, 1975, Massada played in Assen—the provincial city with the largest number of Moluccan youth—at an international pop festival in the local icehockey hall, Triantha. Among the foreign acts on the bill was the popular British souldance band Hot Chocolate. A Dutch television crew filmed the highlights for broadcasting later that summer. After the show a fan by the name of Willem alias Nino Latuny (1943; Jogjakarta, Java) came backstage and asked if he could join Massada as a guitarist.[11] He had toured with former members of The Black Magic in The Hawks. Massada was not looking for a second guitarist but Latuny insisted. After an audition and interview with Zonneveld he was taken on board as rhythm guitarist. Now they were six. On August 2, 1975, Massada was back at the Paradiso.

The Action Years

If anything pointed in the direction of a crisis in Moluccan circles it was the publication in 1975 of the first academic study about the time bomb waiting to go off.[12] The author, Elias Rinsampessy, was an insider. Training as a cultural anthropologist his method was participatory observation. He counted fifty-eight Moluccan quarters in villages and towns all over the country and five remaining barrack camps. The latter were hotbeds of discontent among adolescents. In his summaries of their leisure activities Rinsampessy paid attention to music-making and going out to clubs and discos. He saw a lot of guitars and drums and young men channeling their energy by playing in one or more bands. Clubbing happened in groups that stayed together and avoided intercultural interaction.

The action years had actually started on July 26, 1966, the day Mrs. Josina Soumokil-Taniwel (1934) and her son Thomas Soumokil (1954) had landed at Schiphol Airport, Amsterdam. The execution of her husband, RMS president Chris Soumokil, had taken place on April 12. She was not told where he was buried. An iconic black-and-white press photo shows her coming down the stairs of the airplane holding an electric guitar, her son a few steps behind her.[13] Hundreds of RMS supporters and sympathizers had come to the airport. Unanimously they expressed their commitment to the cause through the battle cry *mena muria*. That night a small group of young RMS followers threw a homemade firebomb at the Indonesian Embassy in The Hague and escaped unnoticed. No one was hurt, but the game had changed.

August 31, 1970, the virtual ninetieth birthday of the deceased Dutch Queen Wilhelmina, was the date of the first action that involved unpremeditated bloodshed. Thirty-three armed Moluccans, all men, all wearing the *berang mera*, the red bandana of the warpath, forced their way into the residency of the Indonesian ambassador in Wassenaar. Their plan was to hold the ambassador hostage and demand the cancellation of the imminent state visit of the Indonesian president Suharto. After fruitless negotiations with the authorities they gave up, walked out, put down their impressive arsenal of modern and traditional weaponry, and were arrested. Three times *mena muria* marked the moment of their voluntary surrender. The action had lasted for twelve hours and cost the life of a Dutch policeman on duty. All but four of the occupants were younger than thirty. They took collective responsibility for the fatal casualty.

Later a poster surfaced with a photo collage of all the men who had participated, the word *Wassenaar* in bright red flames and the RMS emblem on top.[14] The group poses as *pahlawan RMS*, heroes of the South Moluccan Republic. All are casually dressed in western clothes. One of them holds up an electric guitar. The object binds the iconic photograph of Mrs. Soumokil and the *pahlawan* poster. In reality, the occupants at Wassenaar had taken an acoustic guitar with them.

Tete Siahaya had participated in the actions of 1966 and 1970. In jail he wrote a book about the Wassenaar action and his motivation to be an activist.[15] His story touches upon the importance of music in the community. On their way to Wassenaar, cramped in a van with the guitar, they had been singing for courage. Inside the residency they listened to pirate pop stations. In jail they heard noise demonstrations outside, concerts of protest with pots and pans, and Moluccan folksongs. For the first time in Dutch prison history, a music group was permitted to give a performance for the Moluccan inmates. To their utter disappointment, it was an old-fashioned Hawaiian band. Afterward, they filed a written complaint. Next time the *Djodjaros Maluku* (Moluccan Players) lifted their spirits with electric guitars and drums.

Massada was beginning to make a name for themselves in the Dutch club circuit with exciting shows and an increasing number of original compositions when the next action took place. It started on December 2, 1975, and ended on December 19. The trigger had been the proclamation of independence of the Dutch colony Surinam on November 25, 1975, with the full cooperation of the Dutch government. There were two sites. The first was a passenger train held up near the village of Wijster in the north of the country. Three passengers were executed in full view of onlookers. The second site was the Indonesian Consulate in Amsterdam that included a school for children of staff members. One employee was killed.

The Moluccan community formed around 0.03 percent of the population of 13.5 million. Their numbers were too small for anyone not to know someone who knew one of the action takers by name or even personally. Also, Massada carried some of the weight of what had happened. Despite repercussions such as losing bookings and having to endure verbal abuse, they decided to ignore all negative signals and carry on. On December 20, 1975, the day after the voluntary termination of the action, they were back at the Paradiso.

A side-effect of the 1975 action was the attempt to get rid of the colonial term "Ambonese." The matter was a topic at a festival of Moluccan bands swept together under the label *Ambonezenrock* (rock by Ambonese people). Protesters felt it was a term of discrimination, and not in the neutral sense of making a distinction.[16] In the course of 1976, most media switched to calling Massada a South Moluccan band, even though this was more of a political label and did not fit well either. Another side-effect was the use of stronger expressions to describe Massada's performances, such as abundant praise for their perseverance, fierceness, determination, and ability to stir up a storm wherever they went. At the end of the club season 1975–6, Massada was a household name in the scene and beyond and a favorite support act for visiting foreign bands such as The Trammps, Junior Walker and the Allstars, and Osibisa.

At the start of the academic year 1976–7, the Technical University of Eindhoven booked Massada as part of the *Studium Generale* (interdisciplinary program) for students and staff attending the *Lectures on Popular Music* series.[17] Speakers from radio broadcasting organizations and journalists of *Muziekkrant Oor* volunteered their opinions on contemporary pop. Popular music studies as an academic interdiscipline had yet to be theoretically grounded but the first tentative steps had already been taken separately by Dutch and British sociologists. The rumor started to circulate that Massada had already recorded an album and had released singles with predominantly original compositions. Not true but good for keeping the customers curious.

The Dutch keyboard player Frans Eschauzier was the final addition to the permanent line-up. He joined in or around November 1976. Frans was the youngest son of the well-known old-style jazz saxophonist and promotor André Eschauzier whose father had run a sugar cane plantation in the Dutch East Indies. Frans was born in March 1945 in Vught, a small town in the already liberated south of the Netherlands. In 1951 the former concentration camp Vught became a Moluccan relief camp renamed Camp Lunetten. Like in other camps popular music was the bridge to the outside world. At school or in his leisure time Frans may have met Moluccan peers with whom he shared his musical interests. His latest band before Massada was the hard rock supergroup The Flag. He had joined in 1973 and had recorded and toured with them. Eschauzier harmonically cemented the Massada sound, widened the melodic possibilities, and colored the compositions with his latin licks and jazzrock solos. They were now seven and ready to take the next step of their career.

On October 14, 1976, Dutch police forces stormed Camp Berkenoord in Vaassen and ordered the remaining inhabitants to clear the premises. Afterward, the place looked like a war zone. It was the prelude to another armed action. This one involved a passenger train and a primary school. The train was halted on May 23, 1977, at De Punt. At the school in nearby Bovensmilde Dutch and Moluccan children were attending their classes when they were taken hostage together with their teachers. Four days later the children were released. After almost three weeks of fruitless negotiations, special marines forces terminated the action at De Punt in the early hours of June 11, 1977. When the dust had settled, two hostages and six of the nine hijackers were dead. The school was stormed with tanks. No lives were lost there.

Massada was not the only successful Moluccan act in the music industry at this lowest point ever for their community. The singer and songwriter Daniel Sahuleka (1950) whose idol was Stevie Wonder chose to work with Dutch studio musicians and producers. Cheyenne from Oud-Loosdrecht was a navy family's funk band with lead singer Julya Lekranty (1957), a future superstar as Julya Lo'ko. Boozy with Bert Tamaela and Adé Souisa was the revelation of the Groningen disco scene. Like Massada these artists avoided discussions about political issues and focused on their music careers. Unlike Massada they were not integrating Moluccan elements into their music.

After June 11, 1977, Massada stepped up their security measures. Their roadies were prepared just in case a mob would turn against the band for being who they were. That summer Massada played all over the country at music festivals, in holiday resorts, and in discotheques where the disco craze was about to explode. They played the Holland Pop Festival at the Paradiso, headlined the Midsummer Music Fest in Bolsward, were the revelation of the free Zuiderpark Festival in Rotterdam, and outperformed all the bands at the Amsterdam-North music fest in Toni Boltini's Circus.

In the autumn of 1977 Massada made concrete efforts to reach disillusioned Moluccan youth. After a political meeting co-organized by Dutch and Moluccan social workers emotions ran high. Another violent action was promised if the government persisted in ignoring unsolved issues. Massada's music defused the toxicity of the panel discussions. On November 26, Massada was back at the Paradiso to perform at the Latin Festival organized by Latino Promotion in Huizen, an enterprise of the Manuhutu family. Massada and Friends staged a so-called Latin Explosion with all the percussionists that were present. The mother of Johnny and Eppy provided homemade snacks and drinks, a fixed feature of Moluccan hospitality.

On December 17, 1977, Nippy Noya joined Massada at a venue frequented by Moluccan youth in the city of Groningen.[18]

Their support act was American Gypsy, a band of Afro-American musicians from Pasadena who had moved to Spain and then to Maastricht in the south of the Netherlands. From there they toured the Dutch circuit, West Germany, Belgium, and France. Earth, Wind & Fire was their main reference. They already had an album and several singles to their name.

The reviewer on duty that night made the point that Massada bombarded his ears with such complex rhythms that he had lost all orientation. Compared to the show of American Gypsy, projecting the emotional power of soul singing mixed with energizing shots of instrumental funk in compact compositions with singalong bits, he found Massada difficult, chaotic even. How this music would work on record for Dutch ears switched on pop remained to be seen. Massada had been offered recording contracts since their break in 1975, but there were always concessions involved and they had turned them all down. Now they were actually preparing to record.

On March 13, 1978, another Moluccan action took place. It involved the armed occupation of the office building of the provincial administration in the city of Assen. Two bystanders lost their lives. By that time Massada was about to give birth to *Astaganaga*.

Part III
Massada's *Astaganaga*

Massada had been offered recording contracts before, but they had been reluctant to adapt to requirements of accessibility and hit potential, in other words, to play the game of the Dutch music industry. In the early spring of 1978, they signed the deal that resulted in the recording and release, albeit with a hiccup, of *Astaganaga* (Figure 1).

The Making Of

Record company Telstar—named after the US communications satellite launched in 1962—was founded in 1963 by the Rotterdam-born singer, songwriter, talent scout, and producer Johnny Hoes (1917–2011). Telstar had its own production staff, studio, publishing firm, and pressing plant. The firm was located in the south of the country, far from Amsterdam and radio town Hilversum but close to Belgium, West Germany, and Luxemburg, the seat of commercial radio. The boss' daughter Jacqui Hoes (1942–2002) ran the label. She was twenty-one when she started her career in the music business. Core business of the company was recording and releasing old-fashioned song repertoire in the national language or regional

Figure 1 *Massada in Amsterdam in 1978, the year of their debut album Astaganaga. Left to right standing: Frans Eschauzier, Chris Latul, Johnny Manuhutu, Zeth Mustamu, Eppy Manuhutu, Nino Latuny. Front: Usje Sabandar. Photo by Ian Bishop. Collection Latul.*

dialects. For its English language contemporary pop/rock productions Telstar had created the sublabel Killroy.

The signing of Massada entailed the founding of a new sublabel: Kendari Records. The logo consisted of an arrangement of traditional objects associated with Moluccan weddings. Kendari is the name of a settlement on the coast of southeast Sulawesi (formerly Celebes), on the eponymous bay "discovered" in 1831 by the Dutch seafarer and explorer Jacques Vosmaer, hence the colonial name Vosmaer's Bay. Dutch colonizers built Kendari as a probation site for arrested sea pirates who would return to freedom as farmers and fishermen. Over time, it became an important colonial stronghold. During the Second World War, the Japanese invasion of Kendari decimated the Moluccan KNIL-contingent stationed there.

Killroy's label producer Fred Limpens was head of engineering and mixing. Limpens was a performing artist in his own right and a prolific songwriter for mainstream acts signed with Telstar.[1] His co-engineer was Paul Hougardy. In 1977 Hougardy produced the groundbreaking dialect rock band Normaal for Killroy. Recording a latin-rock orchestra was new for both. As their producer Massada had wanted to ask Robert Jan Stips (b. 1950). Stips was a professional keyboardist and composer from The Hague who had worked with Golden Earring and had fronted his own band Supersister. He had recently produced Los Alegres, a latin show trio based in The Hague. Stips happened to be unavailable. An American producer, the only viable alternative as far as Massada was concerned, for budgetary reasons was not an option. So Massada recorded with Limpens and Hougardy in double roles as engineers and producers.

The title of the album holds a story of its own. "Astaganaga" is a Moluccan-Malay exclamation of shock and awe or surprise and admiration or a mix thereof, depending on the occasion, intonation, and facial expression. "Wow!" would be an appropriate translation. The Dutch language has a similar expression: *asjemenou* (pr.: ah-shemme-nao). At the time of *Astaganaga*'s release *asjemenou* was the stopgap of the stuffed puppet lion Loeki—the lion is the Dutch heraldic symbol—that opened and closed the commercial breaks on national television. Loeki was the national mascot, stumbling and fumbling his way through short comical scenes that invariably ended in bewilderment. *Asjemenou* was the slogan of the decade. Dutch fans and buyers did not make the connection, though. To them, the word *Astaganaga*, standing alone as a title without a title track, just looked exotic and mysterious.

All seven core members of the performing group contributed to the recording: Johnny Manuhutu, Eppy Manuhutu, Chris Latul, Nino Latuny, Usje Sabandar, Zeth Mustamu, and Frans Eschauzier. Johnny Manuhutu was credited with lead vocals and percussion. Drummer Eppy Manuhutu also contributed backing vocals and percussion. Nino Latuny played rhythm guitar and acoustic twelve-string guitar and also did backing vocals. Usje Sabandar kept to his bass guitar. Apart from congas, bongos, and timbales, Zeth Mustamu also did backing vocals. Chris Latul was responsible for all lead guitar parts and also did acoustic guitar and vocal parts. Frans Eschauzier played acoustic and electric piano and polymoog (synthesizer) parts.

They were joined by their friend, mentor, and permanent guest star Nippy Noya. Noya brought his latin percussion instruments plus the traditional Afro-Brazilian *berimbau* (a wooden bow with a string attached to it, played with a wooden stick or by hand) and the traditional Moluccan *tifa* (onesided handmade drum of hardwood and animal skin that comes in several shapes and sizes). He was also credited for his "creative fire."[2]

The extra musicians on *Astaganaga* were all carefully chosen. Ronald Ottenhoff was a traverso and saxophone player who had been with the prog rock band Alquin (1971–7), voted Best Dutch Band of 1977 by the readers of *Muziekkrant Oor*. Like Chris Latul, Ottenhoff grew up in Dutch New Guinea. His link with colonial history had filtered into his instrumental composition "New Guinea Sunrise" on the Alquin album *Nobody Can Wait Forever* (1975). Alquin had recorded four albums at the Rockfield Studio in Wales. The fact alone of going abroad to record added to their aura. With their live album, they had delivered the ultimate proof of craftsmanship. When Ottenhoff joined Massada in the studio, he had the status of a rock star.

Keyboard player Hessel de Vries (b. 1947) had been in the public eye since 1969 with the Amsterdam-based supergroup George Cash that featured the Moluccan singer Johnny Frederiksz. Together with Nippy Noya, De Vries had gueststarred with Group 1850, an experimental psychedelic band active between 1966 and 1976, leaving five intriguing albums. Like Noya, De Vries never committed himself to one band only, or one genre for that matter. Before he was asked to contribute to *Astaganaga* he was already well known in the Moluccan music scene where he had worked with, among others, soul singer Jimmy Bellmartin (Jimi Silawanebessy 1949–2021) and rock guitarist Rudy de Queljoe (b. 1947; Surabaya, Java).[3]

Foreign guest musicians were trumpet player Frank Grasso (1949–2020) and saxophonist Harvey Wineapple alias Wainapel (b. 1951). Grasso arranged the horn parts for Wainapel and himself. Both musicians came from the United States and had moved separately to the Netherlands in or around 1973. They worked with Amsterdam-based contemporary jazz ensembles and for radio. Wainapel was a graduate of Berklee NY. His day job was teaching saxophone at the Royal Conservatory of The Hague. Grasso was mainly a jazz man. Wainapel had worked with, among others, Liberation of Man (1975–8), a soul band with an Afro-Caribbean line-up, and the Houseband

(1973–81), a funkrock act featuring the Surinamese-Moluccan singer Monica Tjen A Kwoei. Home of the Houseband was the Paradiso. Massada was not only a household name there, they also found their studio musicians for *Astaganaga* in or via the Paradiso scene.[4]

Track by Track

Side One of *Astaganaga* kicks off with Massada's signature song "Latin Dance" (3'14") written by Zeth Mustamu and arranged collectively. The track explodes into a carnivalesque celebration of vitality. The musical feature that makes the track is the guitar motif. The English lyrics describe the activity of dancing and invite the listeners to join in. English was not in the school curriculum of most of Massada's young fans. The lyrics were not printed on the sleeve either. Therefore the verbal message was easily lost. The rhyming scheme works in pairs, such as trance-dance, sky-shy, and floor-door. Johnny Manuhutu gives soft orders such as "listen to our music and try a latin dance" and gentle reprimands like "don't act as if you're shy."

With these words, Massada addressed a hot topic. Adolescent men in general used to stand in small groups against the walls of clubs and discotheques, watching and looking as if they were waiting for the right moment to join in, but the moment was hardly ever right. The disco craze, at its height when *Astaganaga* came out, sent the unspoken message to Dutch and Moluccan culture of dancing to popular music as a thing for girls and gays. "Latin Dance" tried to push the shy guys over the threshold of their inhibitions.

"Sibu-Sibu" (Seabreeze) (8'07") is a collectively arranged instrumental composition by Chris Latul. The groove is laidback, in a cruising tempo like in Malo's hit "Suavecito" (*Malo* 1972), before changing gear into up-tempo. The track contains memorable melodies and conversational interactions between the melody instruments. Massada's ability to create moods and make interesting transitions from one tempo to the next and from one sound spectrum to the next is a trademark. Sabandar drives the track with his warm melodic bass lines and subtly elastic rhythms.

"Sageru" (3'23") is the most literally Moluccan track of *Astaganaga* and a sure favorite of Massada's live repertoire. The title refers to palm gin, an alcoholic beverage typical for the Moluccan islands. The song is an ode to the traditional drink. The same idea of partying and getting into a trance through dance that runs through "Latin Dance" rules "Sageru". This time Massada ironically adds some "Dutch courage" i.e., alcohol to the recipe. Ottenhoff has a solo traverso part, and the American horn section swings along. The track ends with a concise rhythmic pattern on drums and timbales: a characteristic solution for Massada to intervene in its own musical flow that otherwise could have gone on forever.

This side ends with the equally energetic "NaNaNa Song" (6'54"). The vocals are restricted to "na na na," sung in multipart harmony in a fixed rhythmic pattern with unisono instrumental parts that support the melodic theme. The principle of meaningless syllables as fillers occurred all over popular music. Here Massada may have taken their cue from El Chicano's hit "Tell Her She's Lovely" (1973), which is almost a blueprint of the Massada sound. Several solos give structure and body to the predominantly instrumental track. Wainapel's solo on soprano sax stands out. The horn arrangement exceeds the merely ornamental. Musical fireworks are exploding and note bullets are flying. Around five minutes into the track a percussion break full of "talking" sounds evokes a jungle. The groove holds and the sounds linger for one more minute before returning to the "NaNaNa" theme and ending with clear cut chords in a punctuating rhythm in vintage Massada style, vaguely reminiscent of a marching band setting an exclamation mark.

Side Two begins with the instrumental Massada/Noya composition "Beautiful Berimbau/Sleep My Love" (10'33"), an ode to a mother and child, according to the liner notes. The track evokes tropical landscapes and running streams. The first part is dominated by guitar and keyboards. At 3'30" the track gets into a different groove. Noya plays the traditional berimbau, Latul joins in on guitar through an effect pedal called flanger, we hear all sorts of sounds that emulate the call of tropical birds and the rattle of snakes. A peculiar soundbite from Malo's "Café" (*Malo* 1972) finds its place here in a higher register than its original.

Next is "Dansa (Don't Quit Dancing)" (2'55"), Massada's second single. "Dansa" comes closest to the relaxed groove of old-time mid-tempo latin dance music. The track starts with excited voices as if the musicians are in a club or trying to warm up. Like "Latin Dance" this song has rhyming English lyrics and exhorts the listener who seems unwilling or hesitant to dance. To whom it may concern there is also a word of advice. "Leave your sorrow in the past," Johnny Manuhutu sings, backed by his bandmates. "If you don't know how to do it, we will show you how at last." Near the end the tempo is doubled. Suddenly, there is a sense of urgency. In the fade-out a new guitar theme pops up. The same motif appears in Malo's original version of "Nena" (*Malo* 1972), which is next.

"Nena" (8'37"; Garcia/Téllez) is the only cover on the album. Massada stays close to the original version in the latin boogaloo style also known as latin soul dance. This is the only track on *Astaganaga* that partly has Spanish lyrics (as in the original version). Lines such as "Nena, yo quiero a bailar the boogaloo" and "I want to show you how to dance the boogaloo" are hardly the words of a ballroom teacher at work. Johnny Manuhutu however does not project the song as an exercise in romantic seduction.[5] Near the end the tempo doubles to accompany a jazzy keyboard solo, then switches back to the initial tempo, then doubles again. The strong instrumental licks and short shots of free improvisation that are Massada's trademark find their apotheosis in a resolute final chord.

Sleeve Art and Credits

Everything about the package of *Astaganaga* is carefully credited and everybody involved was a professional in their field. The double outer sleeve is a colorful collage of photograph and drawings that brings together several Moluccan images, symbols, and animistic elements (Figures 2 and 3). The artist, Hans van den Berg, was a friend who owned a graphic design studio in Amsterdam. In the foreground is a cut-out of a photograph of a bride's head and shoulders.[6] She looks away from the spectator at a symbolic depiction of the ancestral home that is left behind. In the background is a pointed

Figures 2 and 3 Back (left) and front (right) image of Astaganaga's fold-out sleeve. Created by Hans van den Berg for Massada. Original in color.

mountain with a fiery glow around the top, representing the volcanic landscape of the home archipelago. In the stream the contours of humans are visible. They represent their ancestors. A hunter looks at the spectator. We see palm trees, plants, flowers, fish, and a partly human butterfly. On the other shore there are two *tifas* with human faces carved out of the wood. We see stilt huts and an *arumbai*. The bridal ornaments are the same as the ones that make up the logo of Kendari Records on the inner sleeve: the fan, the *harkupeng* or hairpins with precious stones on top, the gold or silver comb, and the *bunga tjengkeh* (clove flower).

Credited with the inner sleeve photography of the individual musicians in action is Bob Bunck. Born in Amsterdam in 1950 Bunck was a self-taught press and television still photographer and a visual artist in a variety of disciplines. When he was asked for the job of *Astaganaga* he had already had a couple of well-received exhibitions of his autonomous work in Amsterdam galleries.

Reception and Rewards

On April 28, 1978, Telstar presented the proof pressing of *Astaganaga* at the annual party for music industry and media people at Grand Hotel Krasnapolsky in Amsterdam. Then and there Massada saw and heard their album for the first time. They heard a disastrous mix and noticed that the ranking of the titles on the sleeve did not match the one pressed into the grooves. So they rejected the product and demanded a remix. The company gave them one day to do it. Usje

Sabandar had to do all bass guitar parts again because they had been put on tape at a much too low volume level. The total balance had been set according to the criteria of the music Telstar used to produce. Zeth Mustamu supervised the remix. Massada collectively claimed production credits. On May 15, 1978, the album was officially released, with correct sleeve information.

Record store owners had to figure out how to file *Astaganaga*. Alphabetically under M or perhaps create an exclusive Moluccan category? *Nederlands* (Dutch) suggested Dutch lyrics. *Latijns-Amerikaans* (Latin American) or *Zuid-Amerikaans* (South American) suggested ballroom music. Disco perhaps? The characteristic four-to-the-floor beat was absent. World Music did not even exist as a retail category. In any case *Astaganaga* was a new sound for the Netherlands. Listeners needed time to warm to it.

Muziekkrant Oor planned a review and a background article in its issue of May 17, 1978. Roberto Palombit was put to the task. He had introduced Massada to the readers three years before. From then on he had followed Massada's career. Palombit placed the band closer to the salsa tradition than to the music of Santana. "First and foremost *Astaganaga* is a happy album. It proves that Massada is one of the most promising percussion rock bands. A tropical surprise in a Dutch wrapping," he wrote, alluding to the topical ad of the Bounty Bar brand. The wrapping consisted of the manager, the driving license, and the keyboard player. Inside was the real thing. Joke Zonneveld in the meantime had landed a day job at the Amsterdam-based publishing house of *Muziekkrant Oor*.

Palombit had invited Johnny Manuhutu and Zeth Mustamu to reflect on *Astaganaga*. "A few years ago it would have been impossible to record a song with Malay lyrics," Mustamu said, without explaining any further. Both of them ignored the political circumstances that had made Massada postpone the recording of *Astaganaga* several times. They were pleased to have that all-important calling card for expanding their radius into foreign markets. Mustamu discussed his percussion heroes. Manuhutu promised more songs with lyrics.[7]

At the same time the brand-new Moluccan magazine *Tjengkeh* introduced Massada to its readers in a two-page profile based on a recent interview conducted before the original release date of *Astaganaga*.[8] Johnny Manuhutu did most of the talking. He attributed Massada's success to willpower, discipline, and ambition, qualities he claimed he did not or hardly find in other Moluccan bands. He hoped that *Astaganaga*—which he translated into "far out!"—expressed Massada's South Moluccan identity, albeit in a strictly nonpolitical way, and that it would alert as many people as possible to the situation of the community after all that had happened. "Are there essential differences between a Dutch band and a Moluccan band?" Frans Eschauzier was asked as Massada's only native Dutchman. "Of course!," he replied. "Not only do you play in a Moluccan group, but in fact also an entirely different world opens up to you."

The provincial press of the region where Telstar was based also received *Astaganaga* favorably.[9] The reviewer was pleasantly surprised and used terms like uplifting and refreshing. He found it almost unbelievable that a debut album could be of such high quality. Predicting a great future for the band he gave the album four stars out of five. The popular expression of satirical self-loathing *on-Nederlands goed* (un-Dutch high quality) had so far been reserved for an elite of old-Dutch nationals and their creations. Now it was used for *Astaganaga* and Massada.

"The fact that Massada largely consists of Moluccans has everything to do with the exotic latin-rock that adorns *Astaganaga*," one rock journalist wrote in an Amsterdam newspaper. "Their repertoire sounds a lot like a formation such as Santana."[10] The reviewer alluded to the much-admired ability of Moluccan musicians (in many bands like Massada in the community, not in the limelight) to make the genre their own. Equally important was the fact that Massada tapped into a genre that was popular with a critical mass of Dutch fans. Santana's new album *Moonflower* had just entered the Dutch charts, as had *Astaganaga*. The top position in the meantime was firmly held by the *Original Soundtrack of Saturday Night Fever*. The archetypal disco craze movie was all over Dutch cinemas and fanzines. For a brief moment Santana and Massada were competing within the same market. Santana had the advantage of long-established world fame. Massada was knocking on the door of national fame. Massada outsold Santana.

"Massada has played it cleverly," another national newspaper headlined.[11] The choice of words of its music journalist was quite suggestive. "In cold blood the Moluccan formation Massada has waited for the right moment to penetrate the Dutch Hitparade. With the single 'Latin Dance' and the album *Astaganaga* Massada fights on two fronts and anyone who knows the history of the group will have to admit they have played it cleverly." Johnny Manuhutu did the talking about the history of the group, thus constructing a story the national press and the general public might be able to relate to. Summing up the reasons for Massada's success he mentioned the colonial stereotype of Moluccan military discipline plus the fact that Massada had been a crossover act from the start. He forgot to mention the crucial role of Joke Zonneveld in the process of breaking the barriers of the Dutch rock club circuit outside of Amsterdam.

Avoiding a discussion of the political actions Manuhutu did care to state that Massada and their fans supported a peaceful solution to the given problems of and within the community. He explained Massada's choice for latin music by referring to their own origins in the South Pacific region. The Moluccan mentality came closer to a southern mentality in general than that of the northern people of the Netherlands, he presumed. "I don't want to say that Massada does not feel at home here," he hastened to add. "On the contrary, despite all the trouble it is nice working here."

"Dansa" was the second single taken from *Astaganaga*. The track was released in July 1978 and became a summer hit. Highest position was number fifteen in the first week of August. In the meantime the compilation *Santana Greats* climbed into the album top ten. That same month Massada was the headliner at a three-day open-air fundraising festival for a youth club in Ede, a provincial town with a relatively numerous Moluccan population. On the bill were twenty-one acts, most of them newcomers to the circuit. Massada was kept for last. Due to the exceptionally nice summer weather and a soccer match on tv the turnout was low. *Muziekkrant Oor* had sent a staff member. He was blown away by the professional quality and undaunted attitude of headliner Massada, performing as if they were in front of a full house. In his words, Massada was "the stunner of the evening." His raving review sent a message to readers who had not yet checked the band out: "*Astaganaga* is almost lethargic once you have heard them live. Timing and vim of these people are fabulous. They were the only ones who could get the spectators off their seats."[12]

Hitkrant, the unpretentious counterpart of *Muziekkrant Oor*, around the same time printed its first interview with Massada.[13] The female reporter (an exception to the rule in music journalism of the era) paid attention to the prejudice and negative remarks the band had been receiving in the wake of the Moluccan actions. "Not very nice," was Johnny Manuhutu's reaction, "but we have decided not to worry about that. The most important thing is that the public accepts our music. And that is absolutely the case. *Astaganaga* has reached number five in the album charts. We always go down extremely well live, especially with college students. The venues are always sold out."

On average Massada played five to six times a week. "I have noticed that we have to work ten times as hard as a Dutch act to make progress in the business," said Manuhutu in the same *Hitkrant* interview. "We also have to choose our words very carefully. And when for instance something is missing after the gig, people automatically put the blame on us." To the question whether he was pleased with *Astaganaga* he replied: "Yes, certainly not bad for a debut album. Mostly happy songs with simple lyrics." Eppy Manuhutu agreed: "We want to let the people forget their worries for a couple of hours." For the album they had made their arrangements a bit less "progressive," but that was the only concession they had wanted to make. The real Massada existed to the full in their live shows. The pressing question "Does your music have political influences?" was for Chris Latul to answer: "Absolutely not. Our music exists outside of the political sphere."

At the end of August 1978 *Astaganaga* had disappeared from the Dutch album charts. In September the club season started with Massada as a full-time professional band. The revenues of their concerts not only had to cover their individual costs of living but also the costs of management, promotion, gear, and transport. Very few other bands based in the Netherlands could afford to operate like Massada did. Massada took the working model even further and integrated their entire crew (sound, light, and transport) into their enterprise as equal participants. The idea of collectivism was dominant in the rock and pop band scene but to put it into practice like Massada did was rare.

One booking in particular was interesting for Massada at that point in their career: to open for Santana at the Groenoordhal in Leiden. Santana's *Inner Secrets* Tour of 1978 was taking the famous group to the main venues all over Europe, each time with a local support act.[14] Santana had been scheduled in July. For some reason the concert had to be canceled and was rescheduled for November 17, 1978, at the same venue. With Santana's touring band was the Afro-Cuban star percussionist Armando Peraza (1924–2014). At the last minute, Santana's tour manager decided to fill the support slot with Carlos Santana's experimental jazzrock ensemble The Devadip Orchestra.[15]

A missed opportunity for Massada, for sure. In terms of original compositions, soothing elongated guitar melodies, evocative "talking" percussion, and the occasional surprise of a tropical hailstorm of polyrhythms, engaging the entire orchestra, Massada was second to none at the time of *Astaganaga*. Positive press reviews had given them wings. The facile comparison with Santana had stopped. To critics and fans, Massada came across as an artistic force all its own.

On November 11, 1978, Massada lip-synced "Dansa" on national television. On this occasion Johnny Manuhutu wore a gorilla face mask, perhaps as a reference to the date of the television appearance, traditionally the start of the Carnival festivities when people of all ages put on masks. Or perhaps he alluded to the fact that he was aping his lyrics. There was no way Dutch television would have a band play live on air.

The *Astaganaga*-year went out on a high note. At a party organized by their record company Telstar at the Amsterdam Sonesta Hotel, Massada received a gold record for 50,000 items of the album sold. A photograph and a caption with words of pride and joy for the entire community to share appeared in *Tjengkeh*.[16] Massada also won the Trophy of Best Dutch Band awarded by *Hitkrant*.[17] After ABBA (1976) and Queen (1977), Massada was the third group in line to receive the coveted Trophy. Another popularity poll over 1978 was conducted by the pop/rock radio show *Avondspits* (Evening rush hour), broadcast every working day between six and seven. The show had started in May 1978, just after *Astaganaga*'s date of release. To the inquiry 990 people responded by post and telephone. Most Popular Band of 1978 from the Netherlands was Herman Brood and his Wild Romance with 34.4 percent of the votes. Massada came fourth with 5.3 percent. The top four of the poll were received one by one in *Avondspits*.[18] Massada was on at Christmas Day. On December 28, Dutch television broadcast the *Hitkrant* Trophy Gala in honor of the winners in various categories.[19] By all accounts 1978 had been the year of Massada.

While Massada was touring they were also working on material for the second album. They tried out the new songs and instrumental compositions in their live shows. The new album was due in May 1979, exactly one year after the firstborn. In the run-up to the new release Massada was never lost for new experiences. A rather disappointing one occurred when Massada was contracted as a support act for George Duke on his promotion tour of *Follow the Rainbow*. Now with his own band and repertoire after leaving Frank Zappa's orchestra George Duke was scheduled for two concerts in the Netherlands, one in the Rotterdam theater De Doelen, the other in the Amsterdam Jaap Eden Hall. Massada would do Amsterdam only. It turned out that Duke would not sell enough tickets for both concerts, therefore Amsterdam was canceled and tickets were rebooked for Rotterdam. Massada was not rebooked. Rotterdam went ahead on January 28, 1979, with a considerable number of disappointed Massada fans in the house.[20] On the other hand they were the first to see Duke's twenty-one-year-old percussionist Sheila Escovedo. As Sheila E. she would soon be a star in her own right.[21]

Another experience altogether was opening for The Jacksons on Monday, February 26, 1979, in Theater Carré in Amsterdam. The house was packed with hysterical teenagers dying to see Michael Jackson, already a solo artist with big hits to his name. He drove his fans to fever pitch with his call-and-response routines.[22] Massada used to do the same in "Sageru". In this feature the Black American church and the Moluccan church had similar roots of congregational participation and emotional engagement.

On March 18, 1979, Massada received the *Zilveren Harp* (Silver Harp), the most prestigious national award for a band with a debut album. Massada was now officially recognized as the Most Promising Band of the past year. Nippy Noya joined the magnificent seven at the award ceremony. The publicity picture taken after the ceremony shows them in a pensive mood, hands folded as if in prayer (or boredom). Johnny Manuhutu is the only one with a faint smile. Mustamu wears his raccoon hat in the old-time North American trapper's style that was his trademark.[23] The morning after the award ceremony Massada's record label Telstar congratulated the band and their manager Joke Zonneveld in an ad in the biggest national newspaper *De Telegraaf*.

Two more Dutch musicians had already joined Massada in order to recreate the sound of *Astaganaga* live on stage. Peter Kuyt (trumpet, flugelhorn) and Fred Berkemeier (saxophone) brought the total number of touring musicians up to nine. Depending on the setting of the performance, Massada had developed a live format of one set for attentive listening while seated and one for more active participation, standing, or dancing.[24] In the first set Massada created musically interesting instrumental soundscapes that transcended the conventional song format and depended on the improvisational skills of each individual musician and of the group as a whole. That way a composition never turned out the same. The second set was all about moving to the hits taken from *Astaganaga* and other, as yet unreleased songs for dancing.

When *Muziekkrant Oor* put Massada on the cover of its special issue of April 18, 1979, about popular music made in the Netherlands, the band achieved the equivalent of appearing on the cover of *Rolling Stone*. Anton Corbijn (of later fame as photographer of superstars and as a filmmaker) took the cover picture of Zeth Mustamu, Nino Latuny, and Johnny Manuhutu with the RMS flag wrapped around them. In the background are the barracks of Camp Vught, still partly inhabited by the generation of 1951. On the back cover is an ad for subscribing to *Muziekkrant Oor* and receiving Massada's second album as a bonus. The Dutch word for "subscribe" was changed from *abonneer* to *ambonneer*, using the colonial term all over again as if it had not been contested many times and with valid arguments.

In this special issue Roberto Palombit pitched himself as the ideal person to interview Massada, because he himself was a son of immigrants, in his case from Italy, so he also had the south in him. He let Johnny Manuhutu, Eppy Manuhutu, and Zeth Mustamu give their views on relevant issues, repeat their experiences with discrimination—"in discotheques, they play our records, but we are not allowed in"—and volunteer quite a few clichés about Moluccans. After *Astaganaga* the expectations were high. Palombit had already had the privilege of listening to the mix of the new album and talked through it track by track. Massada was hot, hotter than any other band that made it into the first ever special of homegrown bands in *Muziekkrant Oor*.

The political profiling of the band, albeit superficially, coincided with the first radio broadcast of *Suara Maluku* (The Moluccan Voice) on April 16, 1979. The half-hour-long weekly program of the National Public Broadcasting Organisation had Moluccan presenters and was entirely dedicated to Moluccan news, information, and music. *Suara Maluku* pioneered the field of multicultural media programs by mining the know how and creativity of the community from within. The initiative ran parallel to the spirit of Do-It-Yourself at the anti-commercial margins of youth culture and popular music. It also tied in with the Moluccan tradition of demarcating their playing field and playing that field with their own people.

On April 27, 1979, the national newspaper *Het Vrije Volk* (The Free People) spent an entire page on an interview at Zonneveld's office.[25] "*Het Vrije Volk*, do you hear that, guys, what a beautiful name!," she remarked to break the ice. The hint was not lost on the musicians present. They were open about their thoughts, beliefs, and experiences of being a Moluccan group in the Dutch scene, entertaining full houses, while their hearts and minds were with their own community. For the first time, they talked about their concert the day after the action of 1977 at De Punt had been crushed. They had asked for a minute of silence for "our deceased." Their fans had brought flowers of mourning.

After this emotional moment Johnny Manuhutu, Zeth Mustamu, and Chris Latul returned to the purpose of the interview, the new album. Manuhutu: "We wanted to get rid of the Santana-syndrome people had talked us into. That is why we turned to our own roots more." Mustamu: "The difference [with *Astaganaga*] is day and night. To be honest, the first album doesn't affect me that much, but the second one I am immensely proud of." Latul: "The second album is much more mature, with four solo instrumentalists, and the percussion element less prominent."

Manuhutu played his part as leader of the band when he positioned Massada deeper within the Moluccan fold than they had strategically allowed themselves to do on their rise to the national top. Once there, they felt free to be more specific and speak their minds. "We still have a lot of our Moluccan upbringing inside of us, more than people might suppose," Manuhutu remarked. "The culture that our parents and ancestors have developed over a long time cannot be discarded and replaced from one day to the next. [. . .] The fact that we did not come here by our own choice plays a big role for us. We (our fathers) were forced." The link between the well-known historical facts—Moluccan spokespeople in general tended to repeat the story of their predicament over and over again, presupposing they were not heard or no one understood or cared to know—and the present work of Massada remained to be detected in the new album.

In the meantime *Astaganaga* had sold over 90,000 copies at home and abroad. The album was available in seventeen countries, among others Belgium, France, West Germany, United Kingdom, Switzerland, Ireland, Greece, Turkey, and Surinam. In Indonesia, *Astaganaga* was most likely bootlegged and distributed on audio cassettes. When Nino Latuny had paid a low-key visit to family members on Ambon to his amazement he had been received as a rock star.[26] On April 30, 1979, Queen's Day, Massada reached another popularity peak by playing three concerts at three different locations. It was just two weeks before the release of their second album.

Part IV
Massada after *Astaganaga*

The second album was going to be the all-important proof of Massada's artistic evolution. While the workload increased and the wow factor was wearing off the first cracks appeared. The breakup was front-page news. The reshuffle was the beginning of the end of Massada's time at the top in the industry. The brand survived, as did the music of Massada's unusually challenging early days in the national spotlights.

Bang the Drum

Massada presented their second album *Pukul Tifa* (Bang the Drum) on May 15, 1979, during a sold-out concert in Hilversum, the epicenter of the media and music industry.[1] Nippy Noya guest-starred, as did two female backing vocalists (not credited on the album). True to the Moluccan tradition of hospitality Massada had invited a large number of colleagues in showbiz to an afterparty with plenty of food and drinks. The media had a field day. As for the music of the new album, it indeed displayed a stronger signature style of their own. While the subject matter was more distinctly Moluccan, the music still was anything but traditional.

The sleeve shows all nine musicians with naked upper bodies, shining with oil, in an uneven pyramid formation with Zeth Mustamu on top. For the occasion Nino Latuny has shaven his head in the style of filmstar Yul Brynner. They all wear leather pants and handcrafted ornaments of beads, shells, and metals. A battery of tifas stands in front of them on a bed of hay. The idea behind the picture was to show Massada as a fearsome bunch of precolonial indigenous men of Maluku. No smiles. Cool poses. The photographer was Ronnie Hertz. He had made his name in early 1970s Amsterdam with quasi-erotic photography of female fashion models and was known for talking them out of most of their clothes during the shoot. This time it was Johnny Manuhutu's idea in his quest for an authentic look as Moluccan tribesmen.

Pukul Tifa made the point that the burden of the Moluccan community was also the burden of Massada and to a certain extent also their artistic concern. Lyrically the album was more explicit than *Astaganaga*. The hit single "Unknown Destination" gave Massada an almost pastoral aura of leadership and authority, enhanced by Manuhutu's shouting of "people!" to the imaginary congregation. Musically it was their last farewell to Santana's shadow that had followed them for years. With "Tjakalele" (War Dance) Massada delivered an alternative disco version of an ancient ritual rhythm for getting into a trance. The latter had been the motif of *Astaganaga*'s "Latin Dance", Massada's signature song. With *Pukul Tifa* Massada made a move that may be compared to what bands associated with the *Chicano Power!* movement in San Francisco had done a decade earlier: creating a body of work that stands for the community culture it feeds on. In that sense Massada spearheaded *Maluku Power!* The general public was not aware of the movement, but the community was.[2]

Mission Accomplished

On June 4, 1979, the day after Pentecost Sunday, Massada was the opening act of the international Pinkpop Festival in the sports stadium of Geleen in the south of the country. The slot was reserved for a band based in the Netherlands. More acts were festival-worthy and available, but there was no way around Massada as the recent winner of the award for Most Promising Band. Pinkpop celebrated its tenth anniversary and had put in extra efforts. The sound system of 30,000 watt could reach the far corners of the stadium and beyond. The presenter of the festival was the authoritative BBC radio deejay John Peel.[3]

At eleven o'clock in the morning of what promised to be a tropical day by Dutch standards, Massada opened to a packed festival terrain. Pinkpop had sold 45,000 tickets in advance and would eventually count between 50,000 and 55,000 visitors. A local police spokesperson later estimated a much higher number of around 75,000 visitors. Moluccan youth armed with homemade smoke bombs and bicycle chains tried to force their entrance into the grounds without paying.[4] The incident was swiftly dealt with without Massada even noticing what was happening at the cash point. They ended their set with "Sageru" from *Astaganaga* and exhorted the crowd to join in.

At noon the assembly was properly warmed up for an overall successful festival.[5]

John Peel went on to present The Average White Band from Scotland with their European brand of soul music, followed by Elvis Costello and the Attractions and The Police from England as top exponents of New Wave, the bestselling Dire Straits with their smooth guitar sound, the symphonic hardrock band Rush from Canada and the Jamaican reggae formation led by Peter Tosh. Mick Jagger of the Rolling Stones was expected to join Tosh in the performance of their current duo hit "Don't Look Back", but it was not to be. Instead, Jagger kicked a football around backstage with the musicians of Massada and Tosh.

A few weeks after Pinkpop the biggest national newspaper printed a eulogy by Ad Visser, presenter of Toppop, the Dutch equivalent of the BBC's Top of the Pops. "I would like to congratulate Massada here and now with their excellent career planning, their professional organization and last but certainly not least their well-balanced music," Visser wrote.[6] Referring to *Astaganaga* he heard an album that was not at all the usual sterile product of studio technology but instead sparkled with vitality. The article reads like the jury report of the Silver Harp Award earlier that year. Massada's greatest hit from *Pukul Tifa*, "Arumbai", a laid-back and melodious instrumental composition by Chris Latul, was yet to rise in the charts.

At this point Massada was no longer silent or evasive about burning issues, such as the encounters of Moluccans, in particular adolescent men, with racial discrimination, harassment, and verbal abuse in public places such as cafés and discotheques. Those problems were also their own. *Muziekkrant Oor* reported on the fact that band members were refused entrance to a club while their own music was playing over the sound system.[7] "Not every discotheque owner is charmed by Ambonese, in their eyes not much more than ordinary troublemakers," keyboardist Frans Eschauzier confirmed.[8] "Most venues however continue to book Massada, as you can see in our touring schedule." Although he had spoken of "them" and had used the politically incorrect term "Ambonese," nothing suggested there were frictions in the band.

Being Massada also meant being part of the *National Minorities Show* taking place between June 29 and July 1, 1979, at the RAI, a large industrial hall in Amsterdam. The show was a fundraising event for children in need. Showing up at charity events at their own expense was good for some extra goodwill, so Massada ignored the patronizing frame and approached the gig like any other. To advance their career and not get stuck in the rut of touring the same circuit over and over again Massada needed to cross borders and make new fans.

Hitkrant followed them on their first ten-day tour of West Germany ending in the legendary pop city Hamburg.[9] *Massada Über Alles!* (Massada First!) the magazine printed below a picture of the band members as sophisticated gentlemen. It was a sly reply to the slogan *Hilfe! Die Molukker Kommen* (Help! The Moluccans are coming) used by record company Polydor that represented Telstar in West Germany. The Indonesian ambassador residing in Hamburg had arranged a private concert. In his conversation with the band, he had suggested a tour of Indonesia. The plan leaked and fell through.

Massada continued to branch out in less problematic directions. One of the highlights of the summer of 1979 was their open-air concert on the main square of Brussels on the occasion of the city's 1,000-year anniversary. The festivities were meant to sidetrack the fruitless bickering over issues of language in the Belgian national capital that was also the capital of Flanders. In the wake of the Brussels concert, a team of the Flemish branch of Belgian national television taped Massada's performance in Hasselt at the Cultural Center—a new and more accessible type of theater for contemporary art forms such as cabaret, popular music, modern dance, and musical in Flanders—for broadcasting at a later date.[10] Of the *Astaganaga* repertoire Massada performed "Latin Dance", "Dansa", and "Sageru".

The occasion that may have exposed a certain fatigue within the band was the twelve hours non-stop music event of August 18–19, 1979, at the Triantha hall in Assen. The festival called *Rendez-Vous* was organized by a Moluccan team from Bovensmilde, the municipality near Assen that had been hit hard by the 1977 action. It was promoted as an occasion for Moluccan and Dutch youth to get together and "fraternize." Massada was on the bill with a dozen other bands consisting mainly or entirely of Moluccan musicians and singers. Among the roster was Vitesse, a top-notch power rock band featuring the Moluccan lead guitarist Rudy de Queljoe and the Afro-Surinamese bass guitarist Turu Leerdam. Four to five thousand paying visitors were expected. The revenues would be used to organize another music festival with hopefully also foreign bands in order to raise funds for professional help to young Moluccans in trouble.

The vagueness of the explanation did not satisfy the reviewer of the local newspaper, a Dutch jazz aficionado and early admirer of Massada.[11] On the spot he picked up the rumor that some of the detainees of the 1975 action at Wijster were on unsupervised leave for the first time that weekend. The revenues were supposedly meant for their legal aid and that of others still in detention for the 1975 and 1977 actions. The journalist noticed the disappointing turnout of around 3,000 people, only one in four not Moluccan. So much for fraternizing. Wondering why there had been no traditional music and dance on offer he missed the point that the young generation did not care for a folkloric affair. They were there to see rock bands with great lead guitarists and spectacular rhythm sections. To his amazement the house remained motionless as if frozen, even during Massada's performance. The band was as tight as ever but did not seem as energetic and inspired as the local reviewer remembered them.

In the first week of September 1979 *Pukul Tifa*'s instrumental single "Arumbai" was an alarm disk, which meant that public pop radio played it every hour. At its highest position of number two it beat "Don't Stop Till You Get Enough" by The Jacksons. Massada fake-played it in the television chart show *Toppop* broadcast on September 20. On the day of the broadcast the band had a row and split. Manuhutu informed Joke Zonneveld of the fait accompli. She immediately put all bookings on hold. Messenger to the press was Telstar's head of promotions. *Hitkrant* had the news on the front page of its October 4 issue, as was the case with national newspaper *De Telegraaf*.[12] Speculations galore.

Latul, Sabandar, Eschauzier, and Berkemeier had left. At the center of the disagreement was the issue of total commitment to another five-year plan of hard work at their own and their families' expenses. The leavers received no financial compensation for services rendered, investments made, or royalties due. The remainers—longtime members Eppy Manuhutu, Mustamu and Latuny, and Kuyt—stood with Johnny Manuhutu, the only one left of the founding members. In the first issue of *Hitkrant* after the news had broken, he stepped up his role as bandleader by wishing his former bandmates well and closing the chapter by stating: "I am sorry but I think that we now have the best band possible in this genre." They were already rehearsing with Rudy de Queljoe and Turu Leerdam of Vitesse.

Rudy de Queljoe had first caught media attention with the psychedelic rock group Dragonfly that in 1968 had issued "Celestial Dreams"/"Prince of Amboyna".[13] He had replaced Jan Akkerman (of later world fame as a member of focus and as a solo artist) in Brainbox. With Vitesse he had recorded his composition "Last Boat From Ambon". He joined Massada as one of the top lead guitarists in the scene. He also brought his songwriting skills and his empathy. "The most difficult thing for me right now is to play 'Arumbai'," he told *Tjengkeh* in his first interview as a member of Massada.[14] "It's a big hit at the moment. People have the right to hear the best possible performance of it. It's Chris's composition. His emotions are in it." De Queljoe gave Massada another instrumental anthem called "Mobilae". He had written it on the evening of August 31, 1970, the day of the Wassenaar action.[15]

Turu Leerdam was a leading exponent of the thumping funk style of bass guitar playing in the Netherlands and a songwriter in his own right. With him Massada's drum and bass section gained tightness but lost the melodic approach Sabandar had on his strings. Walter Sell and Jan Stam completed the new Massada on keyboards and saxophone respectively. Sell had an Indo-European background. His former band was Massada's support act Valley Of Dolls featuring the Moluccan percussionist George Louhenapessy. Stam had paid his dues in a handful of bands with and without artistic ambitions. The reshuffle meant the end of Valley Of Dolls. Vitesse continued with Dutch musicians and a different sound. Massada's new line-up rehearsed seven times, did a try-out on October 11, and premiered two days later in the Expo Hall in Hilversum on the same bill as the Golden Earring of "Radar Love" fame. On the last weekend of October 1979 at the Groenoordhal in Leiden, a stage for stars, Massada convinced the last skeptics. All members were now on the same page to make their second five-year-plan result in "perhaps be a global act or something like that," according to De Queljoe in *Tjengkeh*.

Johnny Manuhutu so far did not have a prominent role in the creative side of Massada. He now took to songwriting and arranging. Together with Rudy de Queljoe he wrote "Sajang É" (Feeling pity; 1980) for the annual fundraising event for children in need. The song in the style of a Moluccan traditional was performed by a choir of women and children accompanied by musicians of Massada. It was meant to be a stylistic one-off, a project on the side for the good cause. The single sold so well it landed at number one in the charts in March 1980. By adding it last minute to *Pusaka* (Heritage; 1980), their first studio album with the new line-up, "Sajang É" would go down in history as a Massada hit, their biggest one ever.

Within a year after the breakup, Latul, Sabandar, Eschauzier, and Berkemeier resurfaced in the band Latul. They were joined on a freelance basis by Nippy Noya, Hessel de Vries (guest starring on *Astaganaga*), and other top musicians to form an orchestra as big as Massada and with basically the same musical point of departure as Massada used to have. The Telstar company signed Latul on their Killroy label. Aficionados regarded Latul as the real Massada for stylistic and compositional reasons. To the fans there was only one real Massada. With *Massada Live* (1980) the fresh line-up delivered a master proof of its tightness.

A change of style according to the latest developments in Afro-American funk was the beginning of Massada's descent as a hit group driven by sales figures. The commercial flop of *Baru* (New; 1981), the departure in 1982 of Zeth Mustamu together with Stam, Sell, and Kuyt, a prematurely aborted tour of Indonesia in 1983, more changes of personnel (including their creative anchorman De Queljoe), a record company switch and the lack of airplay caused the end, in 1986, of Massada as a working band.

The spirit of Massada and *Maluku Power!* lingered on in the Moluccan Moods project at the Paradiso. The project consisted of a concert series of up-and-coming bands from the community, while the semi-professional Moluccan Moods Orchestra toured with top musicians and left the eponymous album that marks the first peak of world music made in the Netherlands.

Full Circle

Around the turn of the millennium a rejuvenated Massada with driving force Johnny Manuhutu stepped back into the spotlights.[16] The major events of their second wind were their first concert in Indonesia, at the 2006 Java Jazz Festival in Jakarta, and their emotionally charged first visit to Ambon in 2009 where they were received as long-lost sons. In the Netherlands, Massada became a staple of the rock generation's nostalgia circuit. On June 17, 2011, Massada was back at the Paradiso for a unique integral performance of *Astaganaga* with all original members except Chris Latul.

Between 2011 and 2021 Johnny Manuhutu and Massada have been on a neverending tour with highlights such as the farewell concert for and with Nippy Noya in 2016 and the release of *Baronda* (Out and about; 2018), a double live CD and DVD on the occasion of forty years since the release of *Astaganaga*. The DVD contains footage of their live concert at the Hilversum venue De Vorstin on November 24, 2017, guest-starring Nippy Noya. Of the seven tracks of *Astaganaga* four resurface in live versions on *Baronda*. In the run-up to the seventieth anniversary of the proclamation of the Republic Maluku Selatan RMS on April 25, 2020, Massada would have done several shows had Covid-19 not thrown a spanner in the works.

"We are Moluccans, we play latin music and on stage we look like Indians." This is how Johnny Manuhutu opened a thirty-minute television documentary entitled *Trots op Massada* (Proud of Massada), broadcast on December 4, 2019.[17] This time Chris Latul was invited to participate and contribute his views as a member of the original line-up. The occasion was the belated fortieth anniversary of Massada's legendary performance at the Pinkpop Festival. The documentary also addressed the political issues in the years of Massada's rise to prominence. Manuhutu finally spoke his mind about the actions of the 1970s. "I'd have joined the rebels, if I'd been asked to. Of course!"

In 2021 Johnny Manuhutu had planned to resurface with his first theater tour telling stories about Moluccan traditions and life in exile as he remembers it, with musical intermezzos by Massada's current line-up playing the memorable songs and classic tunes of *Astaganaga* days.[18] That same year Chris Latul wanted to take his new eight-piece latinrocksoulfunkjazz orchestra Latul Lingo Latino on the road, with new compositions and former Massada member Fred Berkemeier.[19] Consecutive lockdowns put both projects on hold until the spring of 2022.

"Ambon—and Maluku in general—is best known for producing Indonesia's top musicans and singers," according to the *Jakarta Post*.[20] The occasion for this praise was the selection of Ambon City, capital of the Indonesian province of Maluku, as a UNESCO City of Music in 2019. The scheme involves cities that "have identified creativity as a strategic factor for sustainable urban development."[21] In order to qualify, creativity must be paired with local cultural industry initiatives, national cooperation, and international exchanges. For Moluccan musicians in the Netherlands the Ambon City of Music umbrella promises to secure a creative connection with the ancestral home.

Hindsight

Massada's rise to national fame occurred at a particularly challenging time for the Moluccan community in the

Netherlands and for the nation at large. Massada had grabbed the spotlights only just before the first of the spectacular actions with fatalities thoroughly changing the context of their work. Massada was put in an awkward position because of who they were. Collective discrimination surged during the second action. Remarkably, the actions had a positive effect on the acceptance of Massada outside of their own community. Because they chose to leave political issues alone and focus on their music for everyone to enjoy, they were embraced by the industry and the media. Because of the rebel stance of their peers in the community, they were embraced by Dutch peers in touch with the zeitgeist in politics and popular music. *Astaganaga* did not explain or solve anything, but it was there at a crucial point in time. According to insiders—Moluccan journalists, historians, and musicians alike—it helped to restore the damaged self-respect of their troubled community in the Netherlands.

The album worked its magic for the music itself, the novelty of the sound, and the unconventional compositions. It contained the band's exuberant signature song "Latin Dance" and cultural anthem "Sageru" next to introvert mood pieces evoking home through tropical soundscapes. Massada had worked for four years to get there. Joke Zonneveld had pushed them hard. She had opened the critical rock circuit for them. She had booked them in places that used to play disco hits and now discovered the sensation of dancing to live music and interacting with the musicians on stage. In a way Joke Zonneveld was to Massada what Leny "Ibu Maluku" Grondel-Chotzen had been to the band of Camp Almere when Johnny Manuhutu was a toddler.

After reaching their first target with the release of *Astaganaga* and all it entailed in terms of artistic recognition and commercial success Massada was in a hurry to outdo *Astaganaga* with a more culturally outspoken and musically more sophisticated follow-up. The wow factor did not repeat itself, though. What remains is an iconic debut album that holds a unique place in the history of popular music made in the Netherlands at a time of crisis in postcolonial affairs and intercultural relations.

Part V
Afterwork

Discography
Studio albums

1978   *Astaganaga* (Kendari Records; Killroy 21006)   LP

Integral rereleases

1990	*Astaganaga*	CD
1994	*Astaganaga* and *Pukul Tifa*	Box set 2 CDs
2008	*De jonge jaren van Massada* *Astaganaga* and *Pukul Tifa*	Box set 2 CDs
2020	*De jonge jaren van Massada* Rerelease of 2008 box set	

Live albums with **Astaganaga** *material newly performed*

1980 *Massada Live* (Kendari Records; LP [taped June 27,
                       Killroy 29005)   1980] "Dansa", "Sageru".
2018 *Baronda*   2CDs + DVD
"Sibu-Sibu", "Latin Dance", "Nena", "Sageru".

Live on compilation albums

2009   *40 Jaar Pinkpop Live*   2 CDs [at Pinkpop Festival 1979]

Compilations including original tracks of Astaganaga

1993   *The Very Best of Massada*   CD
2018   *The Golden Years of Dutch Pop Music: Massada*   2 CDs

DVD

2005   *Massada 25 Years Live*   1 DVD, contains "Dansa",
           (Huizen, June 26, 2004)   "Latin Dance", "Nena", "Sageru".

Cover version/remix of Astaganaga *material*

Marcel Manuhutu (produced by Chris Latul)

1996   "Sageru" (Latin mix   Telstar TS CD 5975-3   single
           /Club mix)

About Research

I conducted my research in the run-up to the seventieth anniversary of the presence of the Moluccan community in the Netherlands (1951–2021). The media paid ample attention to the anniversary through radio interviews, television documentaries, and public zoom discussions. The historical backdrop was freshly laid out with the knowledge of hindsight and recounted from the diverging perspectives of insiders representing four generations. The story had already been told many times from many perspectives, ranging from first-hand experiences with particular aspects to comprehensive political analyses and sociological studies. And yet the anniversary rekindled a seemingly buried trauma. As the year of reminiscing progressed, the media reported about unsolved issues, overdue excuses, court cases, and canceled events. Everything revolved around the historical betrayal that had caused the grudge that had deepened before it exploded in the decade of Massada.

In contrast to the abundance of verified information about the context of my subject, my core subject *Astaganaga* turned out to be uncharted territory. I was free to tackle it any way I saw appropriate. I wanted to understand the iconic quality of this album, the why and how, and who for. The project also fulfilled a promise to myself. During my student years in the 1970s I saw Massada live for the first time, before *Astaganaga* and the media circus that followed. In hindsight, my chance encounter has determined the course of my work as a researcher of homegrown popular music. Postcolonial immigration as a major contributing factor to the creative evolution of popular music produced in the Netherlands became a major theme in my publications. With this volume I return to the band that woke me up to this theme.

Sources and Literature

For digitized newspaper sources and images I turned to the Royal Library of the Netherlands at delpher.nl and to Geheugen van Nederland (Memory of the Netherlands) at geheugen.delpher.nl. The latter includes the collection that used to belong to the Museum Maluku MuMa (1988–2012). I have assembled a concise list of, where possible, English language literature and added a brief description to the Dutch language entries.

Part I Backdrops
Colonial Times and Impact

- Aritonang, Jan Sihar, with Karel Steenbrink eds. (2008). *A History of Christianity in Indonesia* (Studies in Christian Mission 35; Leiden/Boston: Brill). Sheds light on the Dutch campaign of Christianization of the South Moluccas in the nineteenth century entailing the introduction of western music.

- Barker, Ralph (1980). *Not Here, But in Another Place* (London/New York: St. Martin's Press). First-hand journalistic report of the 1970s actions.

- Bouman, Jan C. (1960). *The South Moluccas. Rebellious Province or Occupied State* (The Hague: Sijthoff). Background to legal status of the homelands of the Moluccan community in exile.

- Bosma, Ulbe ed. (2012) *Postcolonial Immigrants and Identity Formations in the Netherlands* (Amsterdam: Amsterdam University Press). Handbook. Contains Fridus Steijlen's chapter "Closing the 'KNIL-chapter': A key moment in identity formation of Moluccans in the Netherlands," 117–35.

- Collected articles (1970, 1975–8) by several authors about the backgrounds and foregrounds of the Moluccan actions in: *Haagse Post Extra*, 1978. In Dutch. Captures the unfiltered atmosphere of the era.

- Decker, Günther (1956). *Republik Maluku Selatan* (Lüneburg: Forschungszentrum für Selbstbestimmungsrecht und Nationalitätenpolitik). In German. First foreign recognition of problematic Moluccan exile. Publication produced by the Research Institute for the Right to Self-Determination and Nationality Policies based in West Germany.

- Herman, Valentine, with Rob van der Laan Bouma (1981) "Nationalists without a nation: South Moluccan terrorism in the Netherlands" in: Juliet Lodge ed., *Terrorism: A Challenge to the State* (New York: St. Martin's Press). Arguably, the first academic publication to include the Dutch situation in international terrorism studies.

- Nightingale, Carl H. (2012). *Segregation, A Global History of Divided Cities* (Chicago/London: The University of Chicago Press). Essential reading for understanding the historical role of the Dutch in using segregation along ethnic and religious lines as a tool to divide and rule the Dutch East Indies.

- Oostindie, Gert (2011). *Postcolonial Netherlands. Sixty-five Years of Forgetting, Commemorating, Silencing* (Amsterdam University Press).

- Smeets, Henk, with Fridus Steijlen (2006). *In Nederland gebleven. De geschiedenis van Molukkers 1951–2006*

[Remained in the Netherlands. The history of Moluccans 1951–2006] (Amsterdam: Bert Bakker). In Dutch. Handbook.

- Utrecht, Ernst (1972). *Ambon. Kolonisatie, dekolonisatie en neo-kolonisatie* [Ambon. Colonisation, Decolonisation and Neo-colonisation] (Amsterdam: Kritische Bibliotheek Van Gennep), tr. from English original to Dutch by Franka Jaspers.

- Van Amersfoort, Hans (2004). "The waxing and waning of a diaspora: Moluccans in the Netherlands 1950–2002" in: *Journal of Ethnic ad Migration Studies*, vol. 30, issue 1, 151–74 (accessible online).

- Vogel, Jaap (2005) *Nabije vreemden. Een eeuw wonen en samenleven* [Close Strangers. A Century of Living Together]. In Dutch. Volume in series: Leo Lucassen and Wim Willems eds. *Cultuur en Migratie in Nederland* [Culture and Migration in the Netherlands] (The Hague: SDU Publishers).

Popular Music in Exile

- Mutsaers, Lutgard (1989) *Rockin' Ramona. Een gekleurde kijk op de bakermat van de nederpop* (The Hague: SDU Publishers). In Dutch. An illustrated history of the introduction of rock and roll in the Netherlands by former inhabitants of colonial Indonesia, including chapters on Moluccan artists.

- Mutsaers, Lutgard (1991) *Moluccan Moods Guitars* (Amsterdam: Multi Music Federation). In Dutch. Booklet accompanying a series of concerts by Moluccan guitarists, with a historical introduction. Multi Music Federation was subsidized by the Dutch Ministry of Education, Culture and Sciences in order to stimulate the visibility of diversity within the popular arts in general and music in particular.

- Mutsaers, Lutgard (1992) *Haring & Hawaii. Hawaiianmuziek in Nederland 1925–1992* (Amsterdam: Mets/SPN). In Dutch. A history of the presence and practice of Hawaiian in the Netherlands, from colonial times into postcolonial revivals, highlighting the important role of Moluccan Hawaiianistas in the 1950s.

- Mutsaers, Lutgard (2000) "Issues of diaspora, community identity and strategic inauthenticity in popular music, featuring the case study 'No more mr. Spice Guy' on Moluccan musicians in the Netherlands" in: Tony Mitchell and Peter Doyle eds. (2000) *Changing Sounds. New Directions and Configurations* (Sydney: University of Technology), 188–94. Conference paper at the IASPM biannual of 1999.

- Mutsaers, Lutgard (2014) *Roep der Verten. Krontjong van roots naar revival* (Haarlem: In De Knipscheer). In Dutch. A history of the mixed western (music) and eastern (lyrics) genre that rose from the Indo-European quarters of 1880s Batavia and developed into the popular music of pre-independent Indonesia.

- Mutsaers, Lutgard, with Gert Keunen eds. (2018) *Made in the Low Countries. Studies in Popular Music* (New York: Routledge). For the bigger picture of popular music made in the Netherlands.

- Roberts, John Storm (1979) *The Latin Tinge. The Impact of Latin American Music on the United States* (Oxford University Press). Essential reading for understanding the global distribution of latin dance music and its fusion with rock, which was a major trend during the formative years of Massada.

Part II Massada before *Astaganaga*

- Bajema, Roeland, with Robert Briel and George Evers eds. (1982) *Nederpop. 25 Jaar popmuziek in Nederland. Compleet overzicht van alle artiesten en hun platen* (Utrecht/Antwerpen: Het Spectrum). In Dutch. Encyclopedia of pop and rock made in the Netherlands. Has an entry on "Massada". Also a source for tracking individual musicians from band to band and supergroup to supergroup in the 1970s.

- Mutsaers, Lutgard (1993) *25 Jaar Paradiso. Geschiedenis van een podium, podium van een geschiedenis* (Amsterdam: Mets/SPN). In Dutch. First quarter century (1968–93) of the Netherlands' most prestigious rock and pop venue. Place where Massada had their decisive break and became a household name. With a list of dates.

- Rinsampessy, Elias (1975) *De mogelijke gronden van agressie onder Molukse jongeren* [The Possible Reasons for Aggression among Moluccan Adolescents]. In Dutch. Paper for Cultural and Social Antropology at Nijmegen Catholic University. Author belonged to the vanguard of Moluccan intellectuals born and/or raised in the Netherlands. Published before the 1975 action took place.

- Steensma, Frans ed. (1990) *Encyclopedie van de Nederlandse popmuziek 1960-1990* [Encyclopedia of Dutch Popular Music 1960-1990] (Amsterdam: Bonaventura) "Massada" 96–7; "Molukken" 101.

- Van Kaam, Ben (1980) *The South Moluccans: Background to the Train Hijackings* (London: C. Hurst & Co.) Updated translation of 1977 Dutch publication *Ambon door de eeuwen* [Ambon through the ages] by the same author (Baarn: Anthos/In den Toren).

Part III Massada's *Astaganaga*

Wikipedia.org, delpher.nl, discogs.com, fan club scrap books, the vaults of *Muziekkrant Oor*, *Hitkrant* and *Tjengkeh*.

Part IV Massada after *Astaganaga*

- Bräuchler, Birgit (2015) *The Cultural Dimension of Peace. Decentralization and Reconciliation in Indonesia* (Palgrave Macmillan Publishers). Sheds light on the causes of the troubles around the turn of the millennium and on the healing process. Provides context for UNESCO's 2019 City of Music scheme for Ambon City and the normalization of collaborations between Moluccans in Maluku and in the Netherlands.

- Spoorman, Rein (2014) "Tradition and creative inspiration: Musical encounters of the Moluccan communities in the Netherlands" in: Bart Barendregt and Els Bogaerts eds., *Recollecting Resonances* (2014 Leiden/Boston: Brill) 281–96. Focus on 1980s (Moluccan Moods project).

Acknowledgments

I thank Fabian Holt of Roskilde University Denmark for inviting me to write a proposal for a volume in this series. Leah Babb-Rosenfeld, Rachel Moore, and Amy Martin at Bloomsbury. Co-readers and advisers Wim Manuhutu, Rocky Tuhuteru, and Eddy Tutuarima. Informants and helpers Zeth Mustamu, Chris Latul, Johnny Manuhutu, Joke Zonneveld, Victor Joseph, Rutger Vahl, Anya Boen, Miranda Klomp, Marcel Goedhart, Jan Maarten de Winter, Bert van Manen, Fred Limpens, Elias Rinsampessy, Robin Freeman, Rob Smaling, Dirk Steenhaut, Frits Spits, and Thijs Gorter.

About the Author

Lutgard Mutsaers (1953) graduated in historical musicology with a focus on theater and dance. Her PhD in cultural history deals with the local impact of international dance crazes. She is a longtime member of the International Association for the Study of Popular Music IASPM and author of monographies, chapters in books, magazine articles, and encyclopedia entries on popular music made in or impacting on the Netherlands.

Notes

Part I

1. Navy personnel was excluded from discharge.
2. Jakob Hoekman (2016) 'Josina Soumokil: mythische moeder van de Molukkers' [Josina Soumokil: mythical mother of the Moluccans] in: *Reformatorisch Dagblad*, March 17. Serge Vinkenvleugel (2018) 'Ik verlang ernaar te weten waar het graf is, voordat ik voor altijd mijn ogen sluit' [I long to know where the grave is, before I close my eyes forever], in: *RTV Drenthe*, July 31, interview Josina Soumokil-Taniwel.
3. Até Latumeten (1978) 'Massada. Astaganaga' in: *Tjengkeh*, May issue. This article in the Moluccan magazine *Tjengkeh* is my source for dates and places of birth of all band members at the time of release of *Astaganaga*.
4. An. (1951) 'Leny Ibu Maluku, de enige ontspanning in Almere' [Leny Ibu Maluku, the sole recreation in Almere] in: *Trouw*, June 16.
5. Lutgard Mutsaers (2021) *Daar bij die molen. Een vergeten artiest en een perfecte soundbite* (Soest: Boekscout) 182. The given example is from 1952.
6. Departure on December 7, 1951, with the Lockheed Constellation PH THD machine 'Arnhem' via Bagdad, Karachi and Manilla to Sydney.
7. https://indo-rock.jimdofree.com/e/electric-johnny-his-skyrockets-rotterdam/.

8 Hans Speekenbrink (2010) 'Steve Boston 75' in: *De Slagwerkkrant*, November–December, 66. In 1982 Steve Boston became the first teacher of latin percussion as a major at the Hilversum Conservatory. In 1979 the Rotterdam Conservatory was the first to integrate latin percussion in its curriculum, with Tito Puente as first artist in residence.

9 Roberto Palombit (1978) 'Noya' in: *Muziekkrant Oor*, August 23.

10 *De Telegraaf*, August 25, 1973.

11 See note 9.

Part II

1 Peter Sijnke and Marcel Koopman (2013) *Kralingen. Holland Pop Festival 1970* (Haarlem: In De Knipscheer).

2 Frank Westerman in his 2016 nonfiction book *Een woord een woord* [A word a word] (Amsterdam: De Bezige Bij) mentions the popularity of Santana among the Moluccan teenagers in his school in the Assen region of the 1970s.

3 An. (1979) 'Massada swingt internationaal' [Massada swings internationally] in: *Amigoe*, 13 July.

4 *De Telegraaf*, September 9, 1971.

5 M. Sopacua, with F.J. Aponno, E. Kaitjily, F. Peletimu and H. Tulusula (1970) *Salawaku R.M.S.* [RMS shield], pamphlet of Vrije Zuidmolukse Jongeren [Free South Moluccan Youth].

6 https://nl.wikipedia.org/wiki/Kamp_Almere.

7 Yigael Yadin (1966) *Masada—Herod's Fortress and the Zelots' Last Stand*, translated in Dutch as: *Masada—Herodes' burcht en het laatste bolwerk der Joden*, published in 1972. In 1973 *Het Nederlands Dagblad* extensively reported on the anniversary.

8 André Nuchelmans (2018) 'Upstart Among the Arts: The Rise of Rock into the Dutch Subsidy System' in: *Made in the Low Countries. Studies in Popular Music* (New York: Routledge) 27–36.

9 *De Waarheid*, February 3, 1975.

10 Roberto Palombit (1975) 'Op safari' [On safari] in: *Muziekkrant Oor* # 6, March 26.

11 *Het Parool*, July 2, 1975, announcement of the festival, 6,000 expected visitors.

12 Rinsampessy 1975.

13 Photograph by Ron Kroon for Algemeen Nederlands Fotobureau ANEFO (General Dutch Photo Bureau). The ANEFO collection is part of the National Archives of the Netherlands and the public domain.

14 https://mollekainama.wordpress.com/links/molukse-acties/ has the poster.

15 Tete Siahaya (1972) *Mena Muria. Wassenaar '70: Zuid-Molukkers slaan terug* [Mena Muria. Wassenaar '70: South Moluccans strike back] (Amsterdam: De Bezige Bij).

16 *Leeuwarder Courant*, April 3, 1976.

17 *Het Vrije Volk*, September 2, 1976.

18 Syp Wynia (1977) 'Massada: aanstekelijke slagwerkfabriek' [Massada: contagious percussion factory] in: *Nieuwsblad van het Noorden*, December 19.

Part III

1. http://nl.wikisage.org/wiki/Fred_Limpens.
2. https://malukuhuizen.nl/adat-muziek.html.
3. Bellmartin won the televised competition *The Voice Senior* in 2018. Unknown to the general Dutch public, he was a longtime star in Moluccan circles.
4. Grasso became a staple of the Dutch jazz scene with his Frank Grasso Big Band and a mentor for jazz students. Shortly after the release of *Astaganaga*, Wainapel left for a job in West Germany. In 1979 he returned to the United States and became a specialist in Brazilian music.
5. The reason may be that street wisdom had taught Moluccan guys not to flirt openly with native girls. Intercultural relationships and marriages were quite common though.
6. The model is Julia Souhoka, married to Massada's drummer Eppy Manuhutu.
7. Roberto Palombit (1978) 'Alleen het rijbewijs is Nederlands... en de manager en de toetsenman' [Only the driving license is Dutch... and the manager and the keyboard player] in: *Muziekkrant Oor* # 10, May 17.
8. Até Latumeten (1978) 'Massada. Astaganaga' in: *Tjengkeh*, May issue.
9. *Limburgs Dagblad*, May 27, 1978.
10. Jim van Alphen in *Het Parool*, June 7, 1978.
11. Ton Olde Monnikhof in *Algemeen Dagblad*, July 11, 1978.
12. Bert van Manen (1978) 'Vele handen maken licht werk' in: *Muziekkrant Oor* # 14, July 12.

13 Irene Scherpenzeel (1978) 'Massada brengt iets nieuws voor Nederland' [Massada brings something that's new for the Netherlands] in: *Hitkrant*, July 20.

14 *De Waarheid*, October 4, 1978.

15 Geert Kistemaker (1978) 'Show Santana professioneel' [Santana show professional] in: *Trouw*, November 20.

16 An. (1979) 'Goud voor Massada' [Gold for Massada] in: *Tjengkeh*, January.

17 *Hitkrant* began in 1974 as an annotated hit list. From January 1977 onward, it was a magazine. In 1978 *Hitkrant* and *Muziekkrant Oor* were sold to the same publisher.

18 Frits Spits (Frits Ritmeester, b. 1948) was the presenter of the show. In 2019 a jury of professional broadcasters pronounced him Most Important Radio Deejay of the Century.

19 Announcement in *De Telegraaf*, December 28, 1978.

20 *Het Vrije Volk*, February 14, 1979.

21 An. (1979) 'Slordige show George Duke' in: *Het Vrije Volk*, January 29.

22 Peter Koops (1979) 'Concert Jacksons: Fris vermaak met perfecte timing' [Jacksons concert: fresh entertainment with perfect timing] in: *NRC*, February 27.

23 The photograph is shown on the Dutch Wikipedia page of Massada: https://nl.wikipedia.org/wiki/Massada_(band).

24 Ben Braber (1979) 'Een avond met Massada' [An evening with Massada] in: *De Waarheid*, February 15.

25 Louis Dumoulin (1979) 'Bekend blijven, daar gaat het om' [To stay famous, that's the challenge; Massada interview] in: *Het Vrije Volk*, April 27.

26 Mentioned by Johnny Manuhutu in the Massada interview of the special of *Muziekkrant Oor*, April 18, 1979.

Part IV

1 Harry van Nieuwenhoven (1979) 'Het Wilde Westen' [review section] in: *Muziekkrant Oor* # 11, May 30, 7.

2 The Moluccan cultural magazine *Tjengkeh* from 1978 onward reported on the musical wave of *latin dendang* (latin percussion) as a dominant genre among Moluccan rockbands.

3 At the time John Peel had a weekly program at BBC Radio 1 and BFBS Radio (British Forces Broadcasting Service) in continental Europe. In the 1980s and 1990s he closely followed the Dutch alternative rock, pop, and dance scene and introduced several local acts to the UK.

4 Regional newspaper *De Limburger* reported the incident (June 5, 1979). The festival site www.pinkpop.org mentioned 75,000 visitors.

5 Stan Rijven (1979) 'Pinkpop festival bijzonder geslaagd' [Pinkpop festival exceptionally successful] in: *Trouw*, 6 June.

6 Ad Visser (1979) 'De moeilijke weg van Massada' [The difficult road of Massada] in: *De Telegraaf*, June 20.

7 Roberto Palombit (1979) "Massada: 'In discotheken draaien ze onze platen, maar zelf mogen we niet naar binnen'" [Massada: "In discotheques they play our records, but we of all people are not allowed in"] in: *Muziekkrant Oor* # 8, April 18, 44–5, 47. Photos by Anton Corbijn. Rudy de Queljoe later wrote 'Discrime' (disco + discrimination) on this topic and recorded it with Massada.

8   Arie van Driel (1979) 'Massada lacht om discriminatie' [Massada laughs about discrimination] in: *Trouw*, 4 July.

9   *Hitkrant*, July 5, 1979.

10 *Limburgse Courant*, January 8, 1980. The concert of Massada in their original line-up and with Nippy Noya was televised that same evening.

11 Eddy Determeyer (1979) 'Verbroederingsfeest trekt voornamelijk Zuidmolukkers' [Fraternization party attracts mostly Moluccans] in: *Nieuwsblad van het Noorden*, August.20.

12 Henk van der Meijden (1979) 'Massada uit elkaar' [Massada split up] in: *De Telegraaf*, October 4.

13 Peter Sijnke (2008) *Dragonfly en de jaren zestig, een tijdsbeeld* [Dragonfly and the 1960s, impression of an era] (Zaltbommel: Aprilis).

14 An. (1979) 'Massada komt met nieuwe formatie' in: *Tjengkeh*, October.

15 Lutgard Mutsaers (2017) *Kaz Lux. Rock-adel verplicht* [Kaz Lux. Noblesse Oblige] (Haarlem: In de Knipscheer). The story of 'Mobilae' told by De Queljoe's friend and musical collaborator Kaz Lux, formerly of Brainbox with Jan Akkerman.

16 Ruud de Graaff (1999) 'Weerzien met Massada' [Rendez-vous with Massada] in: *Fret*, 1 (Amsterdam: Nationaal Pop Instituut), 16–17. Peter Bruyn (2001) 'Massada is terug van weggeweest' [Massada is back from leave], in: *Provinciale Zeeuwse Courant*, September 19, 2001.

17 Hans van Wetering (2019) 'De betekenis van Massada' [The meaning of Massada] in: *VPRO Gids* Week 49, 30–3.

Introduction to tv documentary *Trots op Massada* by Marcel Goedhart.

18 At the time of finalizing this manuscript, all Massada members of *Astaganaga* days except Frans Eschauzier (1945–98) were still around. Guest percussionist Dave Gervais died in 2009.

19 www.latul.com.

20 Gisela Swaragita (2019) "UNESCO names Ambon 'City of Music'" in: *The Jakarta Post*, November 1. The project site www.amboncityofmusic.id accentuates the presumed innate musical talent of Moluccans, a positively self-inflating myth born in the colony and cultivated in the Netherlands. The musicians themselves stay far from essentialist claims.

21 En.unesco.org.

Index

Ambon 5–6, 63, 75–6
Ambonese 9, 35, 61, 69
American Gypsy 39
"Arumbai" 68, 71–2
Assen 20, 32, 39, 70

"Beautiful Berimbau/Sleep My Love" 48
Berkemeier, Fred 60, 71, 73, 76
The Black Magic 15, 32
Boston, Steve 19–20
Bunck, Bob 51

Camp Almere 10–11, 15, 17, 21, 27, 77
Camp Schattenberg 20
Camp Vught 36, 61
Chicano Power! (movement) 25–6, 66
Corbijn, Anton 61

Dakila 25–6
"Dansa (Don't Quit Dancing)" 48, 55, 58, 70
De Fretes, George 13–14
De Queljoe, Rudy 45, 70, 72–4
De Vries, Hessel 45, 73

Disco (genre) 2, 24, 26, 38, 46, 52, 54, 66, 77
Dulfer, Hans 19–20
Dutch East Indies 10–13, 16, 36
Dutch New Guinea 16, 44–5
Dutch West Indies 18, 24

The Eagles (Netherlands) 15, 17, 21, 23–4, 27–8
The Eagles (United States) 27
El Chicano 25, 31, 47
Electric Johnny and His Skyrockets 18
Eschauzier, Frans 36–7, 44, 53, 69, 71, 73

Gervais, Dave 31
Grasso, Frank 45, 47
Grondel-Chotzen, Leny 10–11, 77
guitars 11–19, 23–4, 26, 32–5, 44–6, 48–9, 58, 68, 70–2

Hawaiian (genre) 11–14, 34
Hertz, Ronnie 66
Hitkrant (magazine) 56, 58–9, 69, 71–2

Hoes, Jacqui 41
Hoes, Johnny 41
Hougardy, Paul 43

Indorock-and-roll 14–16, 18

Jazz (genre) 10, 12, 16, 19–20, 36–7, 45, 49, 57, 70, 75–6

Kendari (record label) 42–3, 51
Killroy (record label) 42–3, 74
KNIL (Royal Dutch East Indies Army) 6–7, 16–17, 20, 30, 43
Kuyt, Peter 60, 72, 74

"Last Boat From Ambon" 72
Latin (genre) 17–20, 31, 49
"Latin Dance" 31, 46–8, 54, 66, 70, 77
Latin Explosion 38
Latin percussion 18–20, 23–4, 26–32, 38, 44, 48, 52–3, 57–9, 73
Latin rock (genre) 17, 23, 76
Latul (band) 73–4
Latul, Chris 15–17, 28, 30–1, 44, 47–8, 57, 62–3, 68, 71–6, 78
Latuny, Nino 32, 44, 61, 63, 66, 72

Leerdam, Turu 70, 72
Limpens, Fred 43

Malo (band) 24–6, 47–9
Maluku Power! (movement) 67, 74
Manuhutu, Eppy 27–8, 38, 44, 56, 61, 72
Manuhutu, Johnny 10, 15, 17, 28, 31–2, 38, 44, 46, 48–9, 53, 55–6, 58, 60–3, 66, 71–7
"Mobilae" 72
Moluccan actions 1, 23, 32–5, 37–9, 55–6, 62, 70–2, 76–7
Moluccan folk songs 12, 14, 34
Moluccan islands 5, 6, 8, 27, 47
Moluccan Moods 74
Mustamu, Zeth 30–1, 44, 46, 52–3, 60–2, 66, 72, 74
Muziekkrant Oor (magazine) 23, 31, 36, 44, 52, 55–6, 61, 68

"NaNaNa Song" 47–8
"Nena" 24–5, 49
Noya, Nippy 20–1, 28–31, 38, 44–5, 48, 60, 65, 73, 75

Osibisa 26–7, 36
Ottenhoff, Ronald 44–5, 47

Palombit, Roberto   52–3, 61
Paradiso (venue)   19–20, 23, 29–32, 35, 38, 46, 74–5
pasar malam   7, 14
Pinkpop (festival)   67–8, 75
Puente, Tito   24
Pukul Tifa (LP)   65–6, 68, 71

Republik Maluku Selatan RMS   7–9, 27, 33–4, 61, 75

Sabandar, Usje   15, 28, 44, 47, 51–2, 71–3
"Sageru"   47, 60, 67, 70, 77
"Sajang É"   73
Santana (band)   2, 17, 19, 23–5, 28, 31, 52, 54–5, 57–8, 62, 66
Santana, Jorge   24
Sell, Walter   72–4
"Sibu-Sibu"   47
Soumokil, Chris   9, 33
Soumokil-Taniwel, Josina   33–4
Spice Islands   5, 27

Stam, Jan   72–4
Stips, Robert Jan   43
Suara Maluku (radio)   62

Telstar (record company)   41–3, 51–3, 58, 60, 69, 71, 74
tifa   44, 51, 66
"Tjakalele"   66
Tjengkeh (magazine)   53, 58, 72–3

UNESCO City of Music   76
"Unknown Destination"   66

Van den Berg, Hans   49
Visser, Ad   68
Vitesse   70, 72–3

Wainapel (Wineapple), Harvey   45, 47–8
Wairata, Rudi   13–14

Zonneveld, Joke   29–32, 52, 55, 60, 62, 71, 77